MAHARSHA
ON AGGADOS II
אגדות מהרש״א

Selected Portions

Translated by
Rabbi Avraham Yaakov

YESHIVATH BETH MOSHE
SCRANTON, PA.

TABLE OF CONTENTS

הקדמה

מראש הישיבה

מורינו הרב יעקב שניידמאן שליט"א

חז"ל סידרו האגדות ללמדנו יסודי האמונה והבטחון. והנה הם
בדקדוק גדול בין מצד גוף המימרות ובין מצד סידורם שנקבעים
במסכתא ובפרק הנאות להם כדי להבין עומק הכוונה.

במסכת בבא בתרא בתחלת פרק השותפין שענינו הוא כותל
בחצר השותפין קבעו חז"ל מעשה הורדוס שעסק בתיקון בית שני
ונראה שמזה נבחין ענין בית שני שהוא חלוק במדרגתו מענין בית
ראשון שבית ראשון שרתה בה שכינה והיתה השפעת קדושתה
מלמעלה בגלוי משא"כ בית שני ובפרט סמוך לחורבנה היתה
בחינתה בכותל חצר השותפין שבנוים בין שניהם דהיינו מצד בני
אדם שבנאוה ומצד הקב"ה שהשרה שכינתו בתוכה. והנה בגמ' ראש
השנה דף לא. אמר רב יהודה בר אידי אמר רבי יוחנן: עשר מסעות
נסעה שכינה (פירש רש"י בבית ראשון) וכנגדן גלתה סנהדרין
(פירוש רש"י) בבית שני ובאיארו דבבית ראשון קדושתה היתה מצד
השכינה וכשנחרבה גלתה השכינה, אבל בית שני קדושתה היתה
מצד התורה, וע"י לימוד התורה זכו להוריד הקדושה למטה, ולכן
בחרבנה חלתה הגלות בסנהדרין. ובבבא בתרא דף ד. לאחר שהרג
הורדוס כל החכמים שאל לבבא בן בוטא מה יעשה לתקן חטאו וז"ל
הגמ' השתא מאי תקנתיה דההוא גברא? א"ל הוא כבה אורו של
עולם, דכתיב כי נר מצוה ותורה אור (משלי ו') ילך ויעסוק באורו של
עולם, דכתיב ונהרו אליו כל הגוים (ישעיהו ב') איכא דאמרי הכי
א"ל הוא סימא עינו של עולם דכתיב והיה אם מעיני העדה (במדבר
ט"ו) ילך ויתעסק בעינו של עולם דכתיב הנני מחלל את מקדשי גאון
עוזכם מחמד עיניכם (יחזקאל כ"ד). ופירש המהרש"א דהריגת ת"ח
גרם חסרון בין בגוף התורה ובין בלומדי התורה שיוכלו להורות עפ"י
התורה. וללשון ראשון אמר לו לחדש בנין הבית שיתקן חסרון בגוף
התורה כמו שנא' כי מציון תצא תורה וללשון שני אמר לו שיבנה
הבית לתקן חסרון ת"ח שמורים עפ"י התורה. ונראה ביאורו דאף
שחסרו הרבה ת"ח מ"מ ע"י הסייעתא דשמיא שיש בבית המקדש

ללמוד ולהבין התורה יוכלו להשיג ולהורות כאילו נשארו חכמים רבים.

ונראה דענין זה שביארנו דבית שני היה בגדר בנין בשותפות בינינו ובין הקב"ה, והשראת השכינה היתה רק ע"י לימוד התורה יש בו חסרון ומעלה. יש בו חסרון דהשראת השכינה היתה רק לפי מדרגתנו בלימוד התורה וכן מצינו בבית שני שחסרו חמשה דברים ארון ואורים ותומים ואש העליונה ושכינה ורוח הקדש. אולם יש בו מעלה שהרי אף שנחרבה וגלתה סנהדרין מ"מ לא פסק לימוד התורה מכלל ישראל וזה פועל דעדיין שכינתו בתוכינו ובפרט במקום המקדש ובא"י שמשם יורד ההשפעה לכל העולם. ועיין רמב"ם הלכות בית הבחירה פרק ו' הל' טז' וז"ל אבל חיוב הארץ בשביעית ובמעשרות אינו אלא מפני שהוא כבוש רבים וכיון שנלקחה הארץ מידיהם בטל הכבוש ונפטרה מן התורה ממעשרות ומשביעית שהרי אינה מן ארץ ישראל, וכיון שעלה עזרא וקדשה לא קדשה בכיבוש אלא בחזקה שהחזיקו בה ולפיכך כל מקום שהחזיקו בה עולי בבל ונתקדש בקדושת עזרא השנייה הוא מקודש היום ואע"פ שנלקח הארץ ממנו וחייב בשביעית ובמעשרות על הדרך שביארנו בהלכות תרומה עכ"ל וענין חזקה שכתב הרמב"ם הוא סתום, ואפשר שהוא מטעם שביארנו דהחזקנו בא"י ע"י לימוד התורה שלימודה גרם קדושתה ומכיון שעדיין לומדים התורה עדיין יש בו אותו הקדושה, והיא היא שמחזקת לנו מקום המקדש וכל א"י. ואפשר דיש רמז לזה במשנה ראשונה דבבא בתרא דבסוף המשנה איתא לפיכך אם נפל הכותל המקום והאבנים של שניהם. והיינו דאף דנפל הכותל שמרמז על חורבן הבית והגלות מ"מ המקום והאבנים של שניהם והיינו להקב"ה וישראל שאנו שותפין במקום המקדש. הי"ת יראנו נפלאות מתורתו ונזכה לגאולה שלמה במהרה.

SUMMARY OF
RABBI YAAKOV SCHNAIDMAN'S PROLOGUE

The *Aggados* were recorded by our sages to teach us the fundamental principals of faith and trust. We can derive lessons both from the text and from where the text is recorded.

For example, the first chapter of Bava Basra, which deals with the laws of partners in a courtyard, mentions that Herod refurbished the Second Beis Hamikdash. We can infer from this that the Second Beis Hamikdash was, in a certain sense, like a wall built by partners, for it stood by the grace of Hashem in the merit of Yisrael. This was unlike the First Beis Hamikdash that stood only by the grace of Hashem.

The Gemara in Rosh Hashanna says that the Divine Presence left the First Beis Hamikdash in ten stages, corresponding to the exile of the Sanhedrin, which left the Second Beis Hamikdash in ten stages. This teaches us that sanctity descended on the First Beis Hamikdash because of the Divine Presence, whereas sanctity descended on the Second Beis Hamikdash because of Torah study, which is represented by the Sanhedrin.

The Gemara in Bava Basra says that Herod killed all the Torah sages. Afterwards he repented asking the sage Bava ben Buta, what he could do to atone for his sin. Bava ben Buta answered, "You destroyed the light of the world, therefore involve yourself with building the Beis Hamikdash, which is the light of the world." Others say he answered, "You blinded the eye of the world, therefore involve yourself with building the Beis Hamikdash, which is referred to as the eye of the world." The Maharsha explains that when Herod killed the Torah scholars, he wreaked havoc to the Torah and to the ability of Torah scholars to render Torah decisions. The first opinion in the Gemara is addressing the lack of the

Rabbi Yaakov Schnaidman is the Rosh Yeshivah of Yeshivath Beth Moshe — Scranton, Pennsylvania.

Torah itself. He told Herod to build the Beis Hamikdash, for this brings us the Torah, as it says, *From Zion, the Torah will go forth.* Others felt, that by rebuilding the Beis Hamikdash he rectified the ability of the Torah scholars to render Torah decisions. Perhaps this is because there is Divine Providence emanating from the Beis Hamikdash, which assists Torah scholars to arrive at the proper decision despite the fact that they are few in number.

Being partners with Hashem in bringing sanctity to the Beis Hamikdash, has benefits and demerits. Since the Divine Presence only descends because of our Torah study, when we are lax in our study the Divine Presence is also lacking; indeed our sages tell us that there were five things lacking in the Second Beis Hamikdash. However, despite the fact that the Beis Hamikdash was destroyed, Torah study continued, which causes the Divine Presence to remain amongst us especially in Eretz Yisrael and the place of the Beis Hamikdash.

According to the Rambam, the sanctity that descended on Eretz Ysrael during the First Beis Hamikdash left at its destruction, because this sanctity came through conquest and with its destruction the conquest was nullified. However, the sanctity of Eretz Yisrael gained by the Second Beis Hamikdash did not depart at its destruction, because this sanctity descended on the Second Beis Hamikdash through possession, which was never nullified. It is unclear what the Rambam meant by possession and why it never became nullified. Based on what was previously said, we can surmise that the sanctity that descended on the Second Beis Hamikdash through possession refers to Torah study. Since Torah study continued even after the destruction, its sanctity remained.

The first Mishnah of Bava Basra obligates both partners to build a wall between them. The Mishnah concludes, "Therefore if the wall falls, the place and the stones belong to both of them." Possibly the falling of the wall hints to the destruction of the Beis Hamikdash and our exile. The Mishnah tells us that since the Beis Hamikdash was built through a partnership between the Jewish people studying the Torah and Hashem, the place of the Beis Hamikdash retains its sanctity even while it is destroyed.

May Hashem reveal to us wonders from His Torah, and may we speedily merit the complete redemption.

TRANSLATOR'S INTRODUCTION

Throughout the ages, the moral and ethical teachings of the *aggados* of the Talmud have inspired and uplifted the Jewish people. Interwoven among the halachic deliberations of the Gemara, the *aggados* sparkle with profound wisdom and *yiras Shamayim* (reverence). However, the deeper meaning of the *aggadic* text is often hidden under a mantle of imagery, metaphor, and allegory, so that when taken at face value, many *aggados* may sound implausible.

In his monumental commentary *Aggados Maharsha,* Rabbi Shmuel Eliezer Eidels (1555-1632) offers the key to unlocking the ethical concepts concealed in the allusions, tales, and cryptic sayings of the *aggados*. In that, he follows the counsel of the Rambam: "It is proper to carefully analyze [the *aggados*] . . . when any of these seem far-fetched, we must immerse ourselves in the various branches of knowledge until we understand the underlying ideas" (Introduction to *Peirush HaMishnayos*).

This volume, the second in the series of "Maharsha on *Aggados*," contains selections from a number of tractates, including the famous and fundamental *aggadah* in *Bava Metzia* 59b where G-d performed three miracles to prove the validity of a certain halachah, but was overruled by the Sages who said: "The Torah is not in Heaven."—Concludes *Maharsha:* The Torah was given to man down on earth to decide on the basis of the majority opinion.

Undoubtedly, the most baffling *aggados* in the Talmud are the accounts in *Bava Basra* 73a,b of the bizarre journeys of Rabbah bar Bar Chanah. For example, Rabbah bar Bar Chanah relates how, while sailing aboard a ship, he saw a fish whose back was covered with sand. Thinking it was dry land, he went up and cooked and baked on its back . . . On another journey he saw a bird standing in the water while its head reached the sky. *Maharsha* brilliantly explains the meaning of these perplexing allegories.

In his commentary on *Kesubos* 104a, *Maharsha* analyzes the events surrounding the demise of Rabbi Yehudah Hanassi and explains the seemingly contradictory passages in the Gemara.

In *Taanis* 23a we find the *aggadah* about Choni Hame'agel, the sage who slept for seventy years. *Maharsha* suggests that the seventy years are a reference to the Babylonian exile, which lasted seventy years, and to man's lifespan of seventy years which is nothing but a fleeting dream.

This sampling of *Aggados Maharsha* brings these lofty matters accessible to all to derive lessons from, and gives one a taste of the phenomenal greatness of this sage.

As was mentioned in the introduction to the previous volume, Rabbi Shmuel Eliezer Eidels (Maharsha) was born in Cracow, Poland in 1555; he died in Ostroh, Poland in 1632. As a young man he studied in Posen, Poland, where he married the daughter of Rabbi Moshe Ashkenazi Halpern. He founded a large yeshivah, which was supported for twenty years by his mother-in-law, Eidel. Because of this he is called by her name, Rav Shmuel Eliezer Eidels.

The great kabbalist, Rabbi Yonah Landsdorfer, characterizes the Maharsha's work as follows: "His words are remarkably concise and very profound, and they fathom the true meaning of the Torah. He definitely possessed *ruach hakodesh* (Divine inspiration), without which it would be impossible for a man to write such a work."

It is my hope that the tidbits offered in this volume will whet the reader's appetite to learn Torah from the original text, *lehagdil Torah ul'hadirah.*

AVRAHAM YAAKOV FINKEL
Adar I, 5768/08

SEDER MOED PART II

SEDER NASHIM

SEDER NEZIKIN PART I

MESECHTA PESACHIM

Reward for the Three "Firsts"

———— ❖ ————

PESACHIM 5a

GEMARA: [The Yamim Tovim of Pesach and Sukkos, and the mitzvah of taking the four species, are all associated with the term "first."] As a reward for keeping the three commandments associated with the word "first", Bnei Yisrael will merit three things [designated as] "first". These include, the destruction of the offspring of Eisav, [about which it says, *The first one came out reddish, as hairy as a fur coat* (*Bereishis* 25:25)]; the building of the Beis Hamikdash, [about which it says, *Like the Throne of Glory, set on high from the first, is the place of our Sanctuary* (*Yirmeyah* 17:12)]; and the name of Mashiach, [about which it says, *The first one to come to Tzion [will announce]: "Behold they are here!"* (*Yeshayah* 41:27)].

We are commanded to abstain from work on the first of Pesach, because on Pesach, Bnei Yisrael were freed from

3

those who enslaved them. G-d punished them with various plagues and then drowned them in the sea. In the merit of abstaining from work [on Pesach], Yisrael will be redeemed in the time to come from Eisav, the *first* to oppress us [and the progenitor of Rome, master of our present exile,]. G-d will punish Eisav and destroy his offspring, as the Gemara in Rosh Hashanah (11a) says: "In Nissan they were redeemed, and in the future they will be redeemed in Nissan." Accordingly we clear our homes of all leaven on Pesach, because leaven symbolizes the *yetzer hara* (the evil impulse), which is the spirit of evil and the guardian angel of Eisav, who will be destroyed at the time of the Redemption.

We abstain from work on Sukkos, which is called *first*, because G-d [placed us in sukkos, revealing His *Shechinah* and] spreading His shelter of peace over us, when He took us out of Egypt, as it says, *I had Bnei Yisrael live in sukkos when I brought them out of Egypt* (*Vayikra* 24:42). In the merit of [abstaining from work on Sukkos] we will be rewarded with the rebuilding of the Beis Hamikdash when the *Shechinah* will once again dwell among us, as it says, *Then His sukkah* (i.e., the Beis Hamikdash) *will be in Yerushalayim, and His dwelling in Tzion* (*Tehillim* 76:3).

The mitzvah of *lulav*, is called *first* because it includes rejoicing before Hashem, as it says, *You must take for yourselves on the first day, a fruit of the citron tree, an unopened palm frond . . . You shall rejoice before G-d* (*Vayikra* 23:40). By keeping this mitzvah, Yisrael, will merit rejoicing with the coming of Mashiach, *the first one to come to Tzion.*

The Gemara does not say they will merit Mashiach, rather that they will merit the name of Mashiach, which is Menachem— Comforter. This alludes to the fact that he will comfort us and gladden our hearts, as it says, *Gladden us according to the days You afflicted us* (*Tehillim* 90:15). May this be Your will, speedily in our days, amen.

THE HOUSE OF THE G-D OF YAAKOV

PESACHIM 88a

GEMARA: *And many nations shall go and say,
"Come, let us go to the Mountain of G-d, to the
House of the G-d of Yaakov"* (*Michah* 4:2). Rabbi
Elazar asks, Why will they say, *the G-d of Yaakov*,
and not the G-d of Avraham and Yitzchak? [The
nations will not perceive the Beis Hamikdash], as
the House of the G-d of Avraham, who described
the site of the Beis Hamikdash as a mountain, as
he said, *On G-d's Mountain He will be seen*
(*Bereishis* 22:15). Nor will [they perceive the Beis
Hamikdash] as the House of the G-d of Yitzchak,
who described it as a field, as it says, *And Yitzchak
went out to meditate in the field toward evening*
(*Bereishis* 24:63). Rather they will perceive the
Beis Hamikdash as the House of the G-d of
Yaakov, who described the site of the Beis
Hamikdash as a house, as it says, *[Yaakov] named
the place Beis Keil—the House of G-d* (*Bereishis*
10:19).

The Midrash uses the following allegory to explain this
Gemara: A king, wishing to build a palace, asked three
friends to describe a model after which to pattern his palace. The
first friend said: "I remember [a palace] that looked like a mountain." The second friend said: "I remember [a palace] that remind-
ed me of a field." The third friend said: "I remember an ancient
palace that looked like a house fit for a king." Replied the king: "I
swear that the palace I am going to build will bear your name," for
it says, *The House of the G-d of Yaakov.*

The deeds of the Fathers are an indication for the deeds of their sons. Avraham, the king's first friend, thought of the palace in terms of a mountain, alluding to the first Beis Hamikdash, which was guarded by the *Shechinah*, like a lookout on top of a mountain. Since this guard was not permanent, [it is only referred to as a mountain.] Indeed, the [destruction of] the first Beis Hamikdash is bemoaned, *Mount Tzion which lies desolate* (*Eichah* 5:15).

Yitzchak, representing the king's second friend, suggested a palace that looked like an [empty] field, alluding to the second Beis Hamikdash, which had only minimal protection from Heaven since it lacked many of the holy vessels that graced the first Beis Hamikdash. Indeed the [destruction of] the second Beis Hamikdash is lamented, *Tzion will be plowed over like a field* (*Yirmeyah* 26:18).

Yaakov, the king's third friend, spoke of an ancient palace, referring to the palace that existed before the world was created, which is the everlasting third Beis Hamikdash, may it be built very soon. The third Beis Hamikdash will stand under superior Divine protection as befits a palace, and the nations will call this Beis Hamikdash, the *House of the G-d of Yaakov.*

Waking from his dream, Yaakov said, *This is none other than the House of G-d* (*Bereishis* 28:17). He meant: Since I spent the night here as in a house, this is obviously not a mountain nor a field as my ancestors described it; rather, it will be a [permanent] House of G-d.

COURAGEOUS AS A LEOPARD

PESACHIM 112a

GEMARA: Rabbi Yehudah ben Teima said: Be courageous as a leopard, swift as an eagle, nimble

as a deer and valiant as a lion to do the will of your
Father in heaven.

Rabbi Yehudah ben Teima uses four expressions to denote
diligence because there are four obstacles that prevent a
person from attaining perfection. The first obstacle is poverty, for
the Gemara (Eruvin 41b) says: The pressure of extreme poverty
can force a person to act against [his better judgment and against]
the will of G-d. The second obstacle is decrees imposed by non-
Jewish governments designed to force Jews to abandon their reli-
gion. The third obstacle is the constellation under which a person
is born; indeed the Gemara says, one born in the constellation of
the moon will [have the propensity to] be a thief, and one born in
the constellation of Mars will [have the propensity to] shed blood.
The fourth, and most difficult obstacle, is the *yetzer hara*, the evil
impulse. A person must exert himself to fight these four adver-
saries.

"Be courageous as a leopard," speaks to one suffering from
poverty. He needs courage because he is powerless to change his
situation.

"Be swift as an eagle," urges a person to overcome the adverse
influence of the stars and constellations, just like the eagle, which
flies in the heavens.

"Be nimble as a deer," calls on a person living in times of religious persecution to flee to where he can freely fulfill the mitzvos,
as people did in the days of forced conversions.

"Be valiant as a lion," exhorts a person to fight against his
yetzer hara, as it says: Who is valiant? He who subdues his person-
al inclination (Avos 4:1).

EATING MATZAH ON PESACH

PESACHIM 116B

GEMARA: Why do we eat the matzah? Because the dough that our fathers [prepared to take with them on their exodus from Egypt] did not have time to become leavened before the King of kings, the Holy One, blessed be He, revealed Himself to them and redeemed them, as it says, *And they baked the dough which they had brought forth from Egypt into cakes of matzah, for it was not leavened, because they had been driven out of Egypt and could not tarry, and even provisions they had not prepared for themselves* (*Shemos* 12:39).

This reason is also given in the Haggadah. Accordingly, the mitzvah of eating matzah [at the seder] should be fulfilled after midnight, for that is when Bnei Yisrael departed Egypt, and that is when they baked the dough they brought forth from Egypt! [If so, why do we eat the matzah before midnight? Furthermore, if the matzah commemorates the bread they ate after the redemption,] why were they commanded to eat matzah with the pesach offering, which was eaten before the Exodus? It doesn't seem reasonable to commemorate something that was going to happen in the future!

Possibly, only the prohibition against eating chametz during the seven days of Pesach is to commemorate that the dough they brought from Egypt was baked into unleavened matzah cakes; however, the positive mitzvah of eating matzah the evening of Pesach before midnight, is for the same reason that a meal offering must be eaten as matzah.

Concerning the meal offering it says, *They shall be eaten as ma-*

tzohs in a holy place . . . Any meal-offering that you offer to Hashem shall not be prepared leavened (*Vayikra* 2:11). Our Sages explain, that the leavening in the dough alludes to the *left side,* meaning the *yetzer hara,* which holds us back [from doing the *mitzvos*]. Since the meal offering must be eaten *in a holy place,* which means in a state of *kedushah,* in the environment of the *right side,* as it says, *for it is most holy;* it should not be associated with chametz, which stems from the *left side.*

Just as the meal offering was eaten in holiness as matzah by the kohen, so too, matzah was eaten on the night of Pesach to sanctify all Yisrael, setting them apart from the Egyptians. The night of Pesach is a night of vigil against demons and the forces of the *left side,* which brings us close to G-d, [therefore we eat matzah—the symbol of *kedushah*—on the night of Pesach.] . . .

MESECHTA ROSH HASHANA

TISHREI, THE MONTH OF COMPASSION

GEMARA: Rabbi Eliezer says: In Tishrei, the world was created. In Tishrei, the Patriarchs, [Avraham and Yaakov,] were born; and in Tishrei they died. Yitzchak was born on Pesach. . . . In the month of Nissan we were redeemed from Egypt; and in the future, we will be redeemed in the month of Tishrei.

Rosh Hashanah was fixed on the first of Tishrei, because Adam, [the ultimate purpose of the world,] was created on that day. On that day, Adam was judged for his transgression; he repented and G-d, with the attribute of mercy with which He created the world, forgave him. Avraham and Yaakov were born on this day, which is noted for its attribute of kindness and compassion. This holds a portent for their descendants, that they will be treated with compassion on this day of Judgment.

However, Yitzchak, who represents the attribute of strict justice, was born on Pesach, the Yom Tov on which G-d's attribute of Justice was manifest in the death of the firstborn, and Bnei Yisrael were redeemed through the application of G-d's harsh judgment against the Egyptians.

For this reason we will be redeemed in Tishrei, for in time to come, G-d will look upon Yisrael with boundless mercy, as it says, *With abundant mercy will I gather you in* (*Yeshayah* 8:10). In fact the Gemara derives that in the future we will be redeemed in Tishrei from the verse, *On that day, a great shofar will be blown* (*Yeshayah* 27:13), indicating that the redemption will be through the attribute of mercy, because the sound of the shofar heralds mercy.

The *Omer* and the Two Loaves

rosh hashanah 16a

GEMARA: Rabbi Yehudah in the name of Rabbi Akiva, asked: Why did the Torah command us to bring an *Omer*[1] on Pesach? Since the grain harvest is judged Pesach time, The Holy One, blessed be He, said, "Offer before Me the *Omer* on Pesach, so the grain in the fields will be blessed." Why did the Torah command us to bring an offering of two loaves[2] on Shavuos? Since the fruit of the trees are judged Shavuos time, the Holy One, blessed be He, said, "Offer before Me the two loaves on Shavuos, so the fruit of the trees will be blessed." Why did the Torah command us to pour water [on the Altar] on Sukkos? The Holy One, blessed be He, said, "Pour water before Me on Sukkos, so the rains of this year will be blessed."

---

[1]   The *Omer* offering consisted of a measure of the first reaping of barley, which was offered on the second day of Pesach. Before the bringing of the *Omer*, new cereals of that year were forbidden for use (*Vayikra* 25:10,11).

[2]   On Shavuos, two loaves of wheat flour from the new crop, were brought in the Beis Hamikdash.

Grain, fruit and water sustain the three levels of life; plant life, animal life, and human life. The water poured on the Altar on Sukkos sustains plant life; the *Omer* of barley sustains animal life, as the Gemara (Sotah 16a) says: [The *sotah*] brings a meal offering of barley, which is animal food. The two loaves are from wheat, which sustains human life. Rabbi Yehudah [considers wheat, fruit of a tree,] following his previously stated opinion, that the Tree of Knowledge from which Adam ate, was a wheat stalk, and therefore a child does not acquire understanding until he eats wheat.

This is the meaning of the verse, *When the sickle is first put to the standing crop*—referring to the barley crop, which is brought on Pesach—*you shall begin counting seven weeks* (*Vayikra* 16:9), at which time the wheat is harvested and the two loaves of Shavuos are offered.

This can also be explained on a deeper level. Scripture likens the Egyptians who oppressed Bnei Yisrael to donkeys. Since the Jews had no mitzvos and were on a low spiritual level at the time of the Exodus, they too, were only suited for barley which is animal food. After counting seven weeks and receiving the Torah, they rose to a higher spiritual plane and were ready for the nourishment of wheat, which promotes wisdom. Therefore the two loaves of wheat are brought on Shavuos.

And so the Torah says, *When the sickle is first put to the standing* barley *crop*, which is animal food, *begin counting fifty days*—until the offering of the two loaves of wheat, which is conducive to receiving the wisdom and knowledge of the Torah.

THREE BOOKS OPENED ON ROSH HASHANAH

———✦———

ROSH HASHANAH 16b

GEMARA: Rabbi Kruspedai said: Three books are opened on Rosh Hashanah: one of the totally righteous [people who have more mitzvos than sins], one of the totally wicked [people who have more sins than mitzvos], and one for those in between. The totally righteous are immediately inscribed and sealed in the Book of Life; the totally wicked are immediately inscribed and sealed in the Book of Death; and the sentence for those who fall in between, is left pending from Rosh Hashanah until Yom Kippur. If they become deserving, they are inscribed in the Book of Life; if they don't become deserving, they are inscribed in the Book of Death.

This Gemara gives rise to a question. We see many righteous people die, and many wicked people live in the upcoming year?

This Gemara should be understood in light of the Gemara *Berachos* (18a): The righteous, in death, are called living, and conversely, the wicked, in their life, are called dead. When a righteous man dies, although he passes away from this world, he lives on in the World to Come, however, although the wicked lead an illusory life in this world, they come to absolute extinction in the World to Come. Thus we can understand that a righteous man, whether he lives or dies to atone for his sins in the upcoming year, still lives—either in this world or in the World to Come. Conversely, a wicked man, whether he dies or lives in the upcoming year as a reward for the few good deeds he did, is dead and extinct as far as the World to Come is concerned. That the righteous are written for life on Rosh Hashanah means it is decided which type of life he will be granted in the coming year—life in this world or death in this world in order to attain life in the World to Come. So too, it is decided if the wicked should live in this world to be rewarded for their few good deeds and eventually be punished with eternal death in the World to Come, or receive eternal death immediately. . . .

MALCHUYOS, ZICHRONOS, SHOFAROS

ROSH HASHANAH 32b

GEMARA: [On Rosh Hashanah in the *Shemoneh Esrei* of *Mussaf,*] we recite at least ten verses of *Malchuyos*—verses relating to G-d's kingship; ten verses of *Zichronos*—verses referring to G-d's remembrance; and ten verses of *Shofaros*—verses associated with the shofar.

*M*alchuyos, *Zichronos,* and *Shofaros,* correspond to the three fundamental principles that every Jew is required to believe, namely: G-d's existence; that the entire Torah was given by G-d; and that G-d rewards the righteous and punishes the wicked.

Malchuyos are said to crown G-d as King over us, and all the verses of *Malchuyos* denote His existence and His Oneness.

Zichronos are recited, in order that G-d remember us for good, when He rewards righteousness and punishes sin. The verses of *Zichronos* express this idea.

The verses of *Shofaros* convey the principle that the Torah was given by G-d amid the sound of shofar blasts.

MESECHTA YOMA

YOM KIPPUR IS UNIQUE

GEMARA: Seven days before Yom Kippur the High
Priest was removed from his house . . .

This tractate is called *Yoma*, which means "Day", because Yom
Kippur is the holiest day of the year. The tractate begins with
the word seven, which denotes holiness, since the number seven is
always associated with holiness. Seven is especially apropos to express the holiness of Yom Kippur because its holiness is unique, like
the holiness of Shabbos, which is the seventh day of the week.
Indeed Yom Kippur is called *Shabbas shabbason*, "a sabbath of sab-
baths" (*Vayikra* 23:32), unlike the other *Yamim Tovim,* which are
designated only as *shabbason*. The Torah gives us six days of *Yom
Tov* during the year—one day of Rosh Hashanah, two days of
Pesach, two days of Sukkos, and one day of Shavuos. [These six
days] correspond to the six weekdays, because on these *Yom Tov*
days we are allowed to do labor related to the preparation of food.
But G-d also gave us a seventh Yom Tov day—Yom Kippur—with
a *kedushah* like Shabbos in which every form of labor is forbidden.
Just like Shabbos is a semblance of the World to Come, so too,
Yom Kippur is a semblance of the World to Come—and even more

15

so, for on Yom Kippur, as in the World to Come, there is no eating or drinking. Moreover, Yom Kippur is the only day in the year
on which the Satan cannot bring charges against Yisrael. This is
evident by the fact that the numeric value of *HaSatan*
(5+300+9+50) adds up to 364, one less than the 365 days of the
year, for on Yom Kippur, Satan is incapacitated, just like in the
World to Come where Satan does not exist . . . .

THE MEMORY OF THE RIGHTEOUS
IS A BLESSING

YOMA 38b

GEMARA: Rav Hamnuna said to one of the rabbis
who was setting portions of the Aggadah in order.
What is the basis for the saying: The memory of
the righteous shall be for a blessing? He answered,
"Doesn't it say in Mishlei (10:7), *The memory of
the righteous shall be for a blessing?*" Rav Hamnuna
replied my question is, "What is the source in the
Torah?" The Rabbi answered, "The verse, *G-d
said: 'Shall I hide from Avraham what I am going
to do?'* (*Bereishis* 18:17), is followed immediately
by, *Avraham is about to become a great and mighty
nation, and through him all the nations of the world
will be blessed* (18:18)."

Rav Hamnuna continued, What is the basis
for the saying: The name of the wicked will rot?
The Rabbi answered, from the verse, *The name of
the wicked will rot* (*Mishlei* 10:7). Rav Hamnuna
said, "Where is the source in the Torah?" The
Rabbi answered, "The verse, *Lot pitched tents as
far as Sedom* (*Bereishis* 13:12), is immediately fol-

lowed by, *And the people of Sedom were wicked and sinful* (13:13)."

The Rambam, [when describing the various types of speech,] says: A beloved form of speech is to praise men of exemplary character so people will admire their way of life, and to vilify evildoers so people will have contempt for their misdeeds. This is what is meant when we say, "Remembrance of a righteous one brings blessing, and the name of the wicked will rot".

We say, the remembrance of the righteous brings blessing; yet, we do not say the remembrance of the wicked brings curse. This is because we intend to bless the righteous when we praise their good deeds, however, we do not intend to curse the wicked when mentioning their infamy; rather we hope they will repent, as the Gemara (Berachos 10a) expounds the verse, *Sin will cease from the earth, and the wicked will be no more* (*Tehillim* 104:35). It does not say: "Sinners will cease from the earth," but rather, *Sin will cease from the earth,* because we hope the sinners will repent. The Gemara (Sanhedrin 37a) relates that some outlaws lived in Rav Zeira's neighborhood. Because he showed them friendship they felt remorse and repented. Thus, the name of the wicked decays, for they repent and are no longer called wicked.

Rav Hamnuna searched for sources in the Torah, because having a source in the Torah, makes remembering the righteous a mitzvah. [The source in the Torah for the remembrance of the wicked is,] *Lot pitched tents as far as Sedom* (*Bereishis* 13:12), which is immediately followed by the mention of the disgraceful behavior of the people of Sedom, saying, *Now the people of Sedom were wicked and sinful* (13:13), however the Torah does not curse them. By contrast, when the Torah mentions the righteous Avraham, it praises him, saying, *For I have loved him, because he commands his children and his household* (*Bereishis* 18:19), and continues with a blessing, saying, *Avraham is surely to become a great and mighty nation* (18:18).

THE GREATNESS OF TESHUVA

YOMA 86a

GEMARA: Rabbi Levi said: Great is teshuvah, for it reaches up to the Throne of Glory, as it says, *Return, O Yisrael until Hashem Elokecha* (*Hoshea* 14:2).

Rabbi Levi derives this because according to the context it should have said, "Return O Yisrael to *Hashem Elokecha*,". The word 'until' denotes closeness. He was not able to derive this from the verse, *Let us search and examine our ways and return until Hashem* (*Eichah* 3:40), since in this verse, the prophet mentions only the name, Hashem, without mentioning the name, Elokim [which is a Name of Judgment;] this can be interpreted to mean: "Let us return until His Mercy descends on us," for the name Hashem, denotes divine Mercy. With this in mind, the author of the *tefillah* of the *Yamim Nora'im* composed the phrase: "Let us search our ways and return to You, because Your right hand reaches out to accept those that repent."

How does repentance reach the Divine Throne? It is a known fact that there are heavenly intermediaries between man and G-d. There are accusing angels that prevent a person's prayers from reaching G-d, and there are protective angels that come to a person's defense, bringing prayers before G-d, according to his merit. However there are no intermediaries with teshuvah; teshuvah itself rises straight to the Throne of Glory before G-d Himself, without the help of intermediaries.

MESECHTA TAANIS

THREE WITNESSES

—=◉=—

TAANIS 11a

GEMARA: Anyone who shares in the suffering of the community will merit witnessing its consolation. Perhaps a person [who enjoys himself in the privacy of his home while others are suffering] will say, "Who is there to testify against me?" The stones and beams of a person's house will testify against him, as it says, *For a stone will shout from the wall, and a sliver will answer it from the beams* (*Chavakuk* 2:11).

The yeshivah of Rav Shilah taught: The two ministering angels that accompany each person will testify against him, as it says, *For He will order His angels to you* (*Tehillim* 91:11). Rav Chidka said: A person's own soul will testify against him, as it says, *From the one who lies in your bosom* [i.e., your soul] *guard the doorways of your mouth* (*Michah* 7:5). Others say: A person's own limbs will testify against him, for it says, *You are My witnesses, so says G-d* (*Yeshayah* 43:10).

In regards to all mitzvos the Gemara mentions three witnesses—angels, one's soul, and one's limbs—because there are
three kinds of sins: Forbidden actions; failure to perform a mitzvah;
and forbidden speech.

Two angels will testify against one who performs forbidden
actions, because a person creates angels with his [wrongful] deeds
every day of the 365 days of the year, which correspond to the 365
negative commandments. These [angels] are the troops of the
Angel of Death who is identical with the Satan; in fact the numeric value of *HaSatan* is 364 [5+300+9+50=364], which is 1 less
than the 365 days of the year, for on one day in the year, Yom
Kippur, the Satan cannot bring charges against the Jewish people.
This idea is alluded to in the verse, *He will charge His angels for you,
to protect you in all your ways* (*Tehillim* 91:11). G-d will charge the
angels which one creates with his deeds every day, to protect him
in all his ways, and to testify to [all his deeds].

The Gemara, says: When a person leaves this world, all his
deeds are enumerated before him, and he is asked: Did you do such
and such a thing in such and such a place on such and such a day?
According to this explanation, the angels created by his deeds will
ask these questions.

One who sins through his power of speech, is judged by his
soul because speech comes from the power of the soul, as it says,
*He blew into his nostrils the soul of life, and man became a living
being* (*Bereishis* 2:7). Targum Onkelos translates *a living being* as "a
spirit that speaks." This is derived from the verse, *From the one who
lies in your bosom,* referring to the soul which lies in one's body,
guard the doorways of your mouth, for the soul testifies about the
things one says at the doorways of his mouth.

If someone sins by failing to perform a mitzvah, his limbs give
testimony against him, for the limbs are the tools with which one
performs mitzvos. Thus man has 248 limbs corresponding to the
248 positive commandments he must do. The Gemara cites as
proof the verse, *You are My witnesses, so says G-d* (*Yeshayah* 43:10),
because the previous verse says, *Let them bring their witnesses and*

they will be vindicated (43:9), which the Gemara (Avoda Zarah 2a) interprets to mean, that the mitzvos that Jews do in this world testify on their behalf in the World to Come. In this vein it says, *You,* referring to the limbs of one's body, *are My witnesses,* verifying one's performance of [the mitzvos]. The 248 limbs of one's body will testify whether he did the 248 positive commandments.

PRAYERS FOR RAIN

TAANIS 15a

GEMARA: [On days which we fast for rain, the *chazzan*] recites 24 blessings. These include the eighteen of the daily *Shemoneh Esrei*, and six additional blessings which are: *Zichronos,*[3] *Shofaros,*[4] and [the following psalms]: *In my distress I called upon Hashem* (*Tehillim* 120), *I will lift my eyes to the mountain* (*Tehillim* 121), *Out of the depths have I called You, Hashem* (*Tehillim* 130), *A prayer of the afflicted when he is faint* (*Tehillim* 102).

After each of these six sections a fitting concluding berachah is said. The first section ends with: He who answered Avraham on Mount Moriah, shall answer you and listen this day to the voice of your cry, blessed are You Hashem, who redeems Yisrael.

The second section ends with: He who answered our fathers at the Red Sea, shall answer you . . . blessed are You Hashem, Who remembers that which has been forgotten.

---

3   "Remembrances," i.e., verses describing that G-d remembers man, which are said in the *Shemoneh esrei* of *Mussaf* on Rosh Hashanah.
4   Verses about Shofar blasts said in the *Mussaf* of Rosh Hashanah.

The third section ends with: He who answered
Yehoshua in Gilgal shall answer you . . . blessed
are You Hashem, Who listens to the cry of the
shofar.

The fourth section ends with: He who answered Shmuel in Mitzpah shall answer you. . .
blessed are You Hashem, Who listens to our cry.

The fifth ends with: He who answered Eliyahu
on Mount Carmel . . . blessed are You Hashem,
Who listens to our prayer.

The sixth ends with: He who answered Yonah
in the belly of the fish, . . . blessed are You
Hashem, Who answers in a time of calamity.

The seventh[5] section ends with: He who answered David and Shlomoh, his son, in
Yerushalayim shall answer you and listen this day
to the voice of your cry, blessed are You Hashem,
Who has mercy on the land.

In each of these sections we remember righteous men, and we
pray that in their merit our prayers may be answered just as the
Holy One, blessed be He, answered their prayers with open miracles, changing the course of nature and the laws of the seven days
of Creation, which are represented by the seven planets[6] which op-
pose Yisrael, as our sages tell us that Yisrael does not benefit from
astrological influences. Therefore it says about Avraham, *And He
took him outside and said: "Gaze now toward the heaven, and count
the stars if you are able to count them." And He said to him "So shall
your offspring be!" (Bereishis* 15:5). The phrase *He took him outside*
means that G-d took him out of the hollow space of the world and

---

5   There only six additional berachos, however the first brachah, *Go'el Yisrael*,
"Blessed are You, Hashem, who redeems Yisrael," is always said in the daily
Shemoneh esrei.
6   *Shabsa'i* (Saturn), *Madim* (Mars), *Chamah* (Sun), *Nogah* (Venus) *Kochav*
(Mercury), *Levanah* (Moon), *Tzedek* (Jupiter).

lifted him above the astrological signs of the stars. He said: What do you think? Because Jupiter is in the west you are doomed to be childless? [Of course not. You will benefit from open miracles and be unaffected by the signs of the zodiac.]

The first section mentions Avraham, the first believer [in G-d], whose prayer was answered on Mount Moriah. Avraham did not pray that Yitzchak's life be spared, for [he had said to Yitzchak], *G-d will seek out for Himself the lamb for the burnt offering, my son* (*Bereishis* 22:8). Rather, after Hashem told him not to sacrifice Yitzchak, he prayed that he find an animal for a burnt offering. Possibly Avraham sinned with his subconscious thoughts, therefore he wanted to bring a burnt offering which atones for sinful thoughts. His prayer was indeed fulfilled, for it says, *He saw, and behold, a ram!—another one, caught in the thicket by its horns . . . and he offered it as a burnt offering* (22:13). It says, *a ram—another one*, to teach us that in addition to the ram created during the six days of Creation to be the progenitor of the ram species, a second one was created to be the substitute for Yitzchak. Its ashes are preserved for all future generations [as a remembrance to the merit of the *Akeidah*], therefore this section ends, Blessed are You, Hashem who redeems Yisrael, for the merit of the Akeidah is preserved in every generation.

The second section ends with: He who answered our fathers at the Red Sea shall answer you . . . blessed are You Hashem, Who remembers that which has been forgotten.

This section is inserted because the Holy One, blessed be He, changed the laws of Creation when He split the Red Sea in response to the prayers of Yisrael, as it says, *The children of Yisrael cried out to Hashem* (*Shemos* 14:10).

[Since this berachah speaks about the splitting of the sea which occurred when we were redeemed from Egypt] we says the *Zichronos* as we do on Rosh Hashanah, in order that G-d remember us for good, as He did when He redeemed us from Egypt, as it says, *I will remember for them the covenant of the ancients, those whom I have taken out of the land of Egypt* (*Vayikra* 26:45). The berachah ends: "Blessed are You Hashem, Who remembers forgotten things," because when the Jewish people are oppressed it says, *I have become forgotten as the dead from the heart* (*Tehillim* 31:13), however Hashem will remember us. It says also, *Why do You forget our affliction and oppression?* (*Tehillim* 44:25), which alludes to the suffering of our forefathers in Egypt, as it says, *He saw our affliction, our travail, and our oppression* (*Devarim* 26:7).

The third section ends with: He who answered Yehoshua in Gilgal shall answer you. Hashem answered Yehoshua in Yericho when its seven walls miraculously collapsed. The seven walls represent the astrological powers of the seven planets [which were neutralized.] The *Shofaros* are said in conjunction with this section, because Yehoshua's prayer was answered with the sounding of the *shofar.* Yisrael's prayers on a fast day are also answered with the sounding of the *shofar,* since the Mishnah tells us that during the prayers on a fast day they say, "Blow a T*ekiah!,* Blow a *Teruah!,* Blow a *Tekiah!*" It also says that on a day of war, *you shall blow with trumpets, and you will be remembered before Hashem your G-d, and you will be saved from your enemies* (*Bamidbar* 10:10). The Hebrew word for trumpets is *Chatzotzros,* which can also be read as, *chetzei tzaros*—the arrows of travail; thus we can interpret the verse to read, "you shall blow [the Shofar] when you are beset by travail." Travail is referred to as arrows in the verses, *With My arrows I will destroy them* (*Devarim* 32:23), and, *For Your arrows have been shot at me* (*Tehillim* 38:3). The abovementioned verse ends, *and you will be remembered before Hashem your G-d, and you will be saved from your enemies.*

[Though the sections of *Zichronos* and *Shofaros* are said,] *Malchuyos* is only appropriate on Rosh Hashanah, the day G-d judges the whole world. On fast days, the existence of G-d, which is the theme of *Malchuyos* on Rosh Hashanah, is implied in the section that ends with "Who redeems Yisrael," for that section mentions the promise G-d made on Mount Moriah to Avraham, who proclaimed G-d's existence to the world.

The fourth section ends with: "He who answered Shmuel in Mitzpah," because G-d answered Shmuel's prayer helping Yisrael in a supernatural way, as it says, [*At Mitzpah*] *Shmuel cried out to Hashem and Hashem answered him . . . the Philistines approached for battle with Yisrael. Hashem then thundered them with a great noise on that day and confounded them, in order that they be defeated by Yisrael* (1 *Shmuel* 7:9,10). Then we recite the psalm, *In my distress I called upon Hashem. Hashem, rescue my soul from lying lips* (*Tehillim* 120), because informers in the days of Shaul [and Shmuel] caused them to suffer casualties in war. In spite of this, Shmuel was able to save the Jews in his days through his prayers, as it says in response to the abovementioned prayer, *The hand of Hashem was against the Philistines all the days of Shmuel* (7:13). The psalm ends, *I am peace* (*Tehillim* 120:7). Either Shmuel meant to say: When I was their judge, they had peace from the Philistines, or he may have meant, I peacefully settled their court cases.

The fifth section ends: "He who answered Eliyahu on Mount Carmel," for in response to Eliyahu's plea, *Answer me, Hashem! Answer me!* (1 *Melachim* 18:37), Hashem changed the course of nature, and *a fire descended from heaven and consumed the burnt offering, and the wood, and the stones, and the earth, and licked up the water in the trench* (1 *Melachim* 18:38). We then add the psalm, *I will lift my eyes to the mountain, from where will come my help? My help is from Hashem, Maker of heaven and earth* (*Tehillim* 121). This means: I rely on the merit of the Fathers, who are called "mountains," however, I wonder, *From where will come my help?*, since the merit of the Fathers has been used up. Then I realize, *My help is from Hashem,* and I can only depend on our Father in Heaven. The psalm continues, *Behold, He neither slumbers nor sleeps, the Guardian of Yisrael,* for in the confrontation between Eliyahu and the prophets of Baal, which we mention in this section, *Eliyahu ridiculed them saying, "Cry out in a loud voice, for he is a god! . . . Perhaps he is asleep and he will awaken!"* (1 *Melachim* 18:27). Therefore we mention in contrast, *Behold, He neither slumbers nor sleeps, the Guardian of Yisrael* (121:4). The psalm contin-

ues, *Hashem is your Guardian . . . By day the sun will not harm you,*
in contrast to the famine in the days of Eliyahu.

In the sixth section we recite: "He who answered Yonah in the
belly of the fish . . . ," because G-d answered his prayer, and he
survived supernaturally in the belly of the fish in the depth of the
sea, and was then spit out alive on dry land. We then recite the
psalm, *Out of the depths have I called You, Hashem* (*Tehillim* 130).
This corresponds to Yonah's prayer, *I called in my distress to
Hashem, and He answered me. From the belly of the grave I cried
out—You hear my voice* (*Yonah* 2:3). [When G-d told Yonah to go
to Ninveh and rebuke them for their evil ways,] Yonah ran away,
thinking: If the people of Ninveh repent, it will be an indictment
against Yisrael, who do not pay attention to the words of the
prophets. When G-d repeated the command to go to Ninveh,
Yonah realized he had no choice; therefore he prayed for Yisrael,
saying, *If You preserve iniquities, O G-d, O Lord, who could survive.*
He also prayed that G-d forgive the people of Ninveh should they
repent, saying, *For with You is forgiveness because of this my soul is
afraid.* This would cause *Yisrael to hope to G-d, for with Him is
kindness and abundant mercy so that He will forgive them* (*Tehillim*
130). The psalm ends, *And He shall redeem Yisrael from all its iniquities.* (130:8).

In the seventh section we say: "He who answered David and
Shlomoh, his son, in Yerushalayim, He shall answer you and listen
this day to the voice of your cry." It says in *sefer Tehillim,* that
David prayed for *Yisrael.* Shlomoh also explicitly prayed that no
distress should befall Yisrael, saying, *If your people are defeated by an
enemy . . . If the heavens are restrained and there is no rain . . . If
there is a famine in the land. If there is a pestilence . . .* (1 *Melachim*
ch.8), G-d answered him through fire, which descended from
heaven. The berachah concludes: "Blessed be Hashem . . . Who has
mercy on the Land," because Dovid and Shlomoh's prayers were
that Eretz Yisrael should become inhabited.

LIFE AS A DREAM

———— ◆◉◆ ————

TAANIS 23a

GEMARA: Rabbi Yochanan said: Throughout his life, the righteous [Choni Hame'agel] was troubled about the meaning of the following verse. *A song of ascents. When G-d will return the captivity of Tzion, it will seem to us as a dream (Tehillim 126:1).* Choni wondered, [since the Babylonian captivity lasted seventy years,] how could it be like a dream, for no one can sleep seventy years? Choni once saw a man planting a carob tree and asked him: "It takes seventy years for a carob tree to bear fruit. Are you sure you will live another seventy years to enjoy its fruit?" The man replied: "When I came into the world I found a carob tree that others had planted for me [even though they did not expect to see the fruit of their labor]. Just as my ancestors planted the tree for me, I am planting this tree for my descendants." Choni sat down to a meal, and fell into a deep sleep . . . sleeping for seventy years.

The verse says, *When G-d will return the captivity of Tzion, we will be like dreamers (Tehillim 126:1).* The Babylonian exile lasted seventy years, which is much longer than a dream. However, the verse in *Iyov (20:8),* compares the seventy years of man's life to *a fleeting dream.* Obviously the verse means that the Babylonian exile was as long as the lifespan of a person, which is compared to a fleeting dream.

Choni was bothered that man's entire life should be compared to a fleeting dream without substance. He was shown a man planting a carob tree, which does not bear fruit for seventy years, to teach him that just as a carob tree is barren for seventy years, and then bears fruit, so too, man's life although it is a meaningless dream in this world, he will merit to eat the fruit of his labors in the World to Come. Another possibility is, that although a tzaddik does not benefit from this world, he will merit through his actions, that his children will benefit in this world.

Choni slept for seventy years, indicating that the literal sense of the verse is also true. He was shown the grandson eating the fruits, to verify that indeed the fruits of one's good deeds in this world will be realized after seventy years.

MESECHTA MEGILLAH

FITTING PUNISHMENT

GEMARA: [The *navi* Yeshayah says:] *Your new moons* [Rosh Chodesh] *and your festivals — My soul hates them; they have become a bother to Me* (*Yeshayah* 1:14). Why should [the offering of sacrifices and the celebration of] the new moon and festivals, [even if insincere,] be bothersome? Said The Holy One, blessed be He: Not only does Yisrael sin before Me, they also bother Me [to ponder] what harsh decree to bring upon them [as punishment].

The Gemara explains that the verse does not refer to the celebration of our Roshei Chodashim and Yamim Tovim, but rather to the new month and festival celebrations innovated by Yerovam for idolatrous purposes; indeed these, *My soul hates, they have become a bother to Me*. Yerovam caused the masses to sin by installing golden calves; abolishing the observation of Rosh Chodesh and Yom Tov; and many other sins. The Sages explain that G-d metes out a fitting punishment for every sin, which resembles the sin, so the sinner can recognize that his punishment was indeed exacted by Hashem and did not come by chance. Since Yerovam in-stigated a multitude of sins, they are, so to speak, bothersome to G-d, for He must consider a just and appropriate punishment for each of the many sins.

MESECHTA MO'ED KATAN

A DILIGENT STUDENT

———◦◉◦———

GEMARA: Rabbi Yannai had a student who asked very difficult questions during his daily lecture, but did not ask questions when his Shabbos discourse fell on a Yom Tov [and a large crowd filled the beis midrash]. [In appreciation of the student's thoughtfulness,] Rabbi Yannai applied to him the verse, *To one who evaluates his way, I will show the salvation of G-d* (*Tehillim* 50:23).

Rashi explains that the student did not ask when a large crown was in attendance, in order not to embarrass Rabbi Yannai if he did not know the answer. However it does not seem credible that Rabbi Yannai would not know the answer.

Rashi also explains that the verse, *To one who evaluates his way,* refers to one who calculates the hour when to ask and when not to ask; however this does not fit the text.

We suggest the following explanation: There are two types of talmudic questions: One raises a contradiction to what was said, and the second, wonders if the statement is superfluous.

31

This student questioned many of the statements, "How can we reconcile this statement with another one?" Or, "Why do we need this statement?" However when Shabbos fell on Yom Tov, a large crowd gathered to hear the rabbi's discourse; therefore the rabbi chose a topic adapted to the general public, which was easy and uncomplicated for serious students of the Talmud. Thus the student, who usually challenged Rabbi Yannai during the daily lecture, did not ask questions on this Shabbos since the topic was simple for him. If so, one may wonder, why did he come to the beis midrash at all? Therefore Rabbi Yannai praised him for *evaluating the way,* and calculating the heavenly reward he would receive for walking to the beis midrash. This verse promises that such a person will merit to be shown *the salvation of G-d,* meaning, although he will only hear simple things, Hashem will grant him the ability to see wonders of His Torah from these thoughts.

YOVEL AND *LAG B'OMER*

=====◉=====

MO'ED KATAN 28a

> GEMARA: The death of one who dies . . . at fifty-two years of age, is like the death of [the prophet] Shmuel of Rammah.

*T*osafos quotes the Talmud Yerushalmi that the average life-span of a person is seventy years, as it says, *The days of our years in them are seventy years* (*Tehillim* 90:10). Until twenty years of age, one is considered a minor as far as heavenly punishment is concerned. He is considered an adult, responsible to heaven, for the remaining fifty years.

. . . These fifty years correspond to the years of the *Yovel.* After the twenty years of his youth one must account for all his deeds during the next forty-nine years. During the fiftieth year of his adult life, which is his seventieth year, he reaches his goal and returns to his inheritance, just like the fiftieth year of the Yovel is sanctified and all property returns to its original owners.

From a verse about Shmuel, the Gemara derives that once a person has not sinned for most of his days, he can rest assured that he will continue not sinning (Yoma 38b). In fact this prophecy alluded to Shmuel himself. Because the adult lifespan of a person is fifty years, [one third of a lifespan is sixteen years.] When Shmuel, due to his greatness, died at the age of fifty-two, he had lived the twenty years of his youth plus thirty-two years, which is two thirds of his adult life. Since he reached the majority of his adult life without sinning, it was clear that he would not have sinned the rest of his seventy years.

The fifty-day count of the *Omer* can be understood in a similar fashion. The forty-nine days correspond to the forty-nine years of one's adult life. The fiftieth day is the Holy day of Shavuos. According to the opinion in the Gemara that the world was created in Nissan, [man was created on the first of Nissan, and] the first day of creation was on the twenty-fifth day of Adar, which is twenty days before Pesach. These twenty days symbolize the youth of our forefathers in Egypt, for until the holiday of Pesach they were like minors, not responsible for their actions. Once Pesach and the redemption occurred they became responsible and started the fifty-day count to *Kabbolas Hatorah* and the holiday of Shavuos, which corresponds to the *Yovel* year.

We celebrate the minor holiday of *Lag B'omer* on the thirty-third day of the *Omer* count, for at this point we have reached the two-thirds point in the *Omer*, and the majority of the fifty days have passed. This corresponds to the fifty-second year of one's life, which is comprised of the twenty years of youth and the thirty-two years of adult life, like the life of Shmuel. In fact the word *Yovel* hints to this; its Hebrew spelling is *Yud-Vav-Bais-Lamed*. The numerical value of the first two letters is sixteen, and the value of the last two letters is thirty-two, signifying that there are thirty-two days before and sixteen days after *Lag B'omer* . . .

MESECHTA CHAGIGAH

PILLARS OF THE EARTH

———◆———

CHAGIGAH 12b

GEMARA: Rabbi Yose said: Woe to people, for they see but do not know what they see; they stand but do not know on what they are standing. On what is the earth supported? On pillars, for it says, *Who shakes the earth from its place, and its pillars tremble* (*Iyov* 9:6). The pillars are supported on the waters, as it says, *To Him who spreads out the earth on the waters* (*Tehillim* 136:6). The waters are supported on the mountains, as it says, *Water stands on the mountains* (*Tehillim* 104:6). The mountains are supported on the wind, for it says, *For behold! He forms mountains and creates the wind*. The wind is supported on the storm, for it says, *Stormy wind fulfilling His word* (*Tehillim* 148:8). The storm is suspended from the Holy One, blessed be He, as it says, *And under His arms is the world* (*Devarim* 33:27).

The Sages say: The world rests on twelve pillars, as it says, *He set up the borders of nations parallel to the number [of the twelve tribes] of the children of Yisrael* (*Devarim* 32:8). Others say:

The world rests on seven pillars, as it says, *She carved out its seven pillars* (*Mishlei* 9:1). Rabbi Elazar ben Shamua says: The world rests on one pillar, and its name is *Tzaddik*, for it says, *A tzaddik is the foundation of the world* (ibid. 10:25)

One may ask: Just because people do not know this information, are they to be bemoaned? What is the significance of the number of pillars, whether twelve, seven, or one?

Man was given free will to overcome his *yetzer hara* (evil impulse) with Torah and mitzvos, as the Gemara says: My son, if [the *yetzer hara*,] this despicable creature meets you, drag him into the beis midrash [and start learning Torah], for The Holy One, blessed be He, will help you, as the Rabbis said, "One who comes to cleanse himself, will be helped (Shabbos 104a)." When Rabbi Yose said, "Woe to people, for they see, but do not know what is supporting the world," he meant, they do not realize that man has the ability through his free will, to sustain the world by doing good deeds, or to destroy it by acting sinfully. The world is supported by the choices one makes to keep the Torah and mitzvos, for they are indeed the pillars of the world, as we say: The world depends on three things: Torah study, the service [of G-d], and kind deeds (Avos 1:2). It also says: The world endures on three things: justice, truth, and peace (Avos 1:18). The verse, *Who shakes the earth from its place, and its pillars tremble* (*Iyov* 9:6), means the earth trembles when people do not uphold [the Torah, which is] the pillar that supports it.

The Gemara begins, saying that the pillars are supported by the water. The water refers to the Torah, which is compared to water, as it says *Ho, everyone who is thirsty, go to the water* (*Yeshayah* 55:1).

The water is supported by the mountains, means the Torah was not given to the angels; rather it was given to the tzaddikim who are likened to mountains, as it says, *The voice of my Beloved! There he comes, leaping over mountains, bounding over hills* (*Shir Hashirim* 2:8).

The mountains are supported on the wind, means the tzaddikim who choose to do good, depend on the wind, which is their
pure soul, as it says, *He blew into his nostril the soul of life* (*Bereishis*
2:7).

All this depends on man's choice to subdue the storm wind,
which is the *yetzer hara;* as the Gemara says that *Iyov* referred to the
yetzer hara as a storm wind... This storm wind can be subdued if
one makes an effort to cleanse himself, for when he does so, the
Holy One, blessed be He, helps him. Thus the storm [the *yetzer
hara*] is suspended from the arm of the Holy One, blessed be He,
who helps one who chooses to conquer his *yetzer hara.*

Rabbi Yose does not mention on how many pillars the world
rests, relying on the Mishnah that mentions three pillars: Torah,
service of G-d, and kind deeds. However the other sages follow the
Gemara, *Makkos* (24a), which says that although there are 613
mitzvos, David reduced this number to eleven fundamental
mitzvos. Yeshayah condensed them to six fundamental principles.
Michah condensed them further to three fundamental principles.
Finally Chavakuk condensed them to one underlying principle,
faith, as it says, *The tzaddik shall live through his faith* (*Chavakuk*
2:4). Following this pattern, the Sages said the world rests on
twelve pillars, which are the eleven fundamentals of David plus
faith. The sages who said there are seven pillars, follow the view of
Yeshayah who counted six fundamental mitzvos; including faith
there are seven fundamentals. Rabbi Elazar ben Shamua said the
world rests on one pillar, referring to faith, which is the one fundamental mitzvah mentioned by Chavakuk. He called this pillar
tzaddik, because Chavakuk mentioned the mitzvah of faith regarding the *tzaddik,* as it says, *The tzaddik shall live through his faith.*
This is the reason he said, *A tzaddik is the foundation of the world,*
for through his faith he supports the world. This is also the meaning of the verse, *Your faithfulness is from generation to generation,
You established the earth and it endures* (*Tehillim* 119:90), for faith
is the single pillar on which the world rests.

Teaching Torah to a non-Jew

---◆◆◆---

CHAGIGAH 13a

GEMARA: Rav Ammi said: The teachings of the Torah should not be transmitted to a non-Jew, for it says, *He relates His Word to Yaakov, His statutes and judgments to Yisrael. He did not do so for any other people; such judgments—they do not know them, Halleluyah!* (*Tehillim* 148:20).

[T]osafos asks: What portions of the Torah does Rav Ammi mean? He cannot be referring to the seven Noachide laws,[7] for it is a mitzvah to teach gentiles these laws so that they perform them. And in regard to teaching them the rest of Torah , we do not need Rav Ammi's prohibition, for we have learned that a non-Jew who studies Torah is liable, and a Jew who teaches him violates the prohibition of aiding one to sin.

If we examine Rav Ammi's words, he did not say that Torah may not be taught to a non-Jew, rather he said, that the teachings of the Torah should not be transmitted to a non-Jew]. We may surely teach a non-Jew the seven Noachide commandments [which non-Jews are required to observe], and if a non-Jew learns the other mitzvos of the Torah, he bears guilt for his soul.

However, transmitting Torah, means teaching the Torah in depth. A non-Jew should not be taught the reasons and mysteries of the mitzvos, even those of the seven Noachide commandments. As proof, the Gemara cites the verse, *He relates His Word to Yaakov, His statutes and judgments to Yisrael*—G-d revealed the reasons for

---

[7] The seven Noachide commandments are: (1) To establish courts to administer social justice. To avoid: (2) blasphemy; (3) idolatry; (4) adultery; (5) murder; (6) robbery; (7) eating flesh cut from a living animal.

His statutes and judgments to Yisrael; *He did not do so for any other people*—for even when it comes to their social legislation, and establishing courts of justice which is one of the seven Noachide mitzvos, *they do not know them*—they do not know the deeper reasons and mysteries of these laws.

MESECHTA KESUBOS

YISRAEL UNDER G-D'S SUPERVISION

━━━━◉━━━━

KESUBOS 66a

GEMARA: Rabbi Yochanan ben Zakkai said: "How praiseworthy is Yisrael! When they do the will of G-d, no nation or people has power over them, but when they fail to do the will of G-d, He delivers them into the hands of a depraved nation, and not only into the hands of a depraved nation, but into the hands of the beasts of a depraved nation."

R abbi Yochanan ben Zakkai praises Yisrael when they do the will of G-d and the nations are powerless over them, and also when they fail to do His will, and the nations rule over them. [What is praiseworthy about being ruled by the nations when we don't do G-d's will?]

Actually both instances reflect the praiseworthiness of Yisrael, for every other nation has a guardian angel and a sign of the zodiac [that determines its fate]. However, Yisrael's destiny is not set by the signs of the zodiac nor by a guardian angel, rather, *His own nation remains Hashem's portion, Yaakov is the lot of His heritage* (*Devarim* 32:9). [Yisrael relies only on G-d's direct and close

39

supervision.] Therefore, when Yisrael does the will of G-d, they transcend all nations and guardian angels, as it says, *Hashem took Avraham outside and said: "Look at the sky and count the stars. See if you can count them." [Hashem] then said: "This is how numerous your descendants will be"* (*Bereishis* 15:5). The Sages explain the passage *Hashem took Avraham outside* to mean Hashem placed him above the heavenly constellations [making him immune to the influence of the signs of the zodiac]. But when Yisrael does not do the will of G-d, He removes His *Shechinah* from them, and [without a guardian angel to rely on,] they become inferior and more despised than all the other nations, which have guardian angels.

RABBI YEHUDAH HANASI'S DEATH

KESUBOS 104a

GEMARA: On the day that Rebbi (Rabbi Yehudah Hanasi)[8] died, the Rabbis declared a public fast, praying for mercy. They said: Whoever says Rebbi died, will be stabbed with the sword.

Rebbi's maidservant went to the roof and prayed: "The angels desire Rebbi, and the mortals desire Rebbi. May it be the will of G-d that the mortals overpower the angels." But when she saw how Rebbi suffered, . . . she prayed: "May it be the will of G-d that the angels overpower the mortals." Because, the Sages prayed continuously, preventing Rebbi from dying, she threw an earthenware jar from the roof to the ground, momen-

---

8   Rabbi Yehudah Hanasi, also called Rabbeinu Hakadosh or Rebbi compiled the Mishnah, an achievement that earned him the undying gratitude of the Jewish people. The Gemara testifies: "From Moshe until Rabbi Yehudah HaNasi we do not find Torah and Majesty combined in one person" (*Sanhedrin* 36a).

tarily distracting them from their prayers. At that moment, Rebbi's soul departed.

The Sages sent Bar Kappara to see how Rebbi was faring. Upon entering the room he saw that Rebbi had passed away. He tore his garment, turning the tear to the back [so that no one would see it] and returned, saying: "The angels and the tzaddikim took hold of the holy Ark [i.e., Rebbi]. The angels overpowered the tzaddikim, and the holy Ark was captured." The Sages asked him: "Do you mean he passed away?" [Not wanting to contravene the directive of the sages and say Rebbi had died] he answered, "You said it, I never said it."

When Rebbi passed away he raised his ten fingers and said: "Master of the universe, it is known to You that I toiled studying the Torah with my ten fingers, yet I did not enjoy worldly pleasure even with my little finger. May it be Your will that there will be peace in my final resting place." Thereupon a Heavenly Voice came forth, declaring, "*He will come in peace; they shall have rest on their beds—he who walks in his integrity*" (*Yeshayah* 57:2). The verse uses the plural, *on their beds,* rather than the singular, "on his bed", . . . to teach us that when a tzaddik leaves this world, the angels say before The Holy One, Blessed is He, "This tzaddik is coming." Hashem answers, "Let the tzaddikim greet him." They say to him, "*He will come in peace; they shall have rest on their beds."*

Rabbi Elozor said: When a tzaddik departs the world, three groups of ministering angels proclaim before him. One group says, *Come in peace.* The second group says, *He who walks straightforward.* The third group says, *He will come in peace; they shall have rest on their resting places.*

When a wicked person is removed from the world, three groups of destroying angels greet him. The first group says, *There is no peace for the wicked, said Hashem* (*Yeshayah* 48:22). The second group says, *From My hand has this [decree] come upon you, that you should die in sorrow* (*Yeshayah* 50:11). The third group says, *Descend and be laid to rest with the uncircumcised* (*Yechezkel* 32:19).

This Gemara gives rise to a number of questions:

Why did the Rabbis object to announcing that Rebbi died, more so than other great Rabbis?

Why did they eventually announce themselves: "Rebbi has passed away"?

What is meant by, "the angels desired Rebbi"?

Why does the Gemara mention the type of jar the handmaid threw from the roof?

Bar Kappara referred to Rebbi as the Ark, saying: "The angels and the tzaddikim took hold of the holy Ark, and it was captured." Why didn't he refer to Rebbi as the Torah, saying, "the Torah was captured"?

Why did Rebbi mention that he toiled in Torah with his ten fingers, rather than with his entire body?

Why does the Gemara question the plural of *their beds* and not the plural of *they will rest* [which is in the same verse]?

Man is a composite of soul and body. Man's thoughts are a function of his soul while his actions are a function of his body. Rebbi was completely perfect in both his Torah study and his fulfillment of the mitzvos, for which reason he was called *Rabbeinu Hakadosh*. [Because of his saintliness,] he could have lived forever. Furthermore, Rebbi suffered many ailments all his life, enduring pain for the sake of his generation, as the Gemara says: During the years that Rebbi suffered, the world did not need rain [for everything grew without rain] (Bava Metzia 85a). Since he could have lived forever and because he protected the generation, the Rabbis decreed: "Whoever says Rebbi died will be stabbed with the sword."

Rebbi's maidservant said, "The angels desire Rebbi," because his soul belongs to the world of the angels—the World to Come—where one can attain complete perfection in Torah learning. Mortals also desired Rebbi in this world, because he could attain complete perfection by doing mitzvos and living forever with body and soul. However when she saw that his physical body was failing him, causing him to suffer and have difficulty with his tefillin, she realized that it could not attain complete perfection, so she prayed: "May it be the will of G-d that the angels overpower the mortals."

When the Rabbis continued praying, preventing Rebbi from dying, she threw an earthenware jar from the roof, hinting, that just as a broken earthenware pot cannot be repaired, so too, once a man's body is broken and wracked with pain he cannot attain perfection through mitzvos, as was evident through Rebbi's difficulty in putting on tefillin. . . .

Bar Kapparah referred to Rebbi's death as the capture of the holy Ark, rather than the capture of the Torah, because one's Torah, which represents his intellect rooted in his soul, is not removed from him in this world nor in the World to Come. However his physical body, represented by the holy Ark, does indeed die and enter the grave, and is "captured" from this world.

When Rebbi passed away he raised his ten fingers, because when one dies, he loses the ability to perfect himself through actions which depend on his physical body. However, intellectual perfection comes through the power of the soul, which will be strengthened in the World to Come. Fingers are the primary limbs for physical activity; since Rebbi perfected his actions by following the Torah during his lifetime, he asked that his physical body find peace in its final resting place.

Although the verse uses the plural expression twice—*they will rest,* and *on their beds*—the Gemara does not question the expression, *they will rest,* because this refers both to the peaceful rest of the body in the grave and the soul in the World to Come, where the soul attains complete perfection. However the term *on their beds,* refers specifically to the grave, and we cannot say the soul enters the grave. Thus the Gemara answers, when a tzaddik dies, the other tzaddikim greet him and they too will have peace in the grave.

The three groups of ministering angels that proclaim before the tzaddik, come from the upper world, the intermediate world, and the lower world. The angels from the upper world say, *He will come in peace,* because peace reigns in the upper world of the Divine family [of angels], and that is where the soul of the tzaddik is bound in the Bond of Life. The angels of the intermediate world say, *He who walks straightforward,* for in this world the tzaddik walks straightforward negating the influence of the stars which control this world, and from here comes the spirit of man. The angels of the lower world, say, *They shall have rest on their beds,* for in this world the body is buried.

However, when an evildoer dies and is erased from the world, the angels from the upper world say, *There is no peace for the wicked, said Hashem (Yeshayah* 48:22). Those from the intermediate world say, *From My hand has this [decree] come upon you, that you should die in sorrow (Yeshayah* 50:11). The angels from the lower world say, *Descend and be laid to rest with the uncircumcised (Yechezkel* 32:19).

MESECHTA NEDARIM

LEARNING FOR THE SAKE OF TORAH

━━━━●《◎》●━━━━

NEDARIM 62a

GEMARA: Rabbi Eliezer bar Tzadok said: Perform mitzvos for the sake of their Maker, and speak of them for their own sake, [not for the sake of reward]. Do not make the Torah a crown for self-glorification, nor a spade with which to dig. This follows from logical reasoning: Belshatzar used the holy vessels after they lost their sanctity and was uprooted from the world; surely a person who uses the crown of Torah [whose sanctity is everlasting, for his own purposes, will be destroyed]!

The Gemara lists four things which motivate people to learn Torah and perform mitzvos. Two of them are commendable—[performing mitzvos for the sake of their Maker, and, speaking of them for their own sake]—and two of them are reprehensible—[making the Torah a crown for self-glorification, and a spade with which to dig].

The four motivations to learn Torah and do mitzvos can be easily memorized by the acronym אגדל (*alef, gimel, dalet, lamed*);

for each of these letters [when spelled out] contains the letter *lamed*, which can be translated as "to learn."

The letter *alef*, [which translates as master,] refers to one who learns so people should call him "my rebbi and master."

The *gimel*, [which translates as reward,] alludes to one who learns for the sake of *g'mul*, "the reward in the World to Come."

The *dalet*, [which translates as door,] stands for one who uses learning as a gate toward earning a livelihood.

The *lamed*, [which translates as learning,] refers to one who learns for the sake of G-d, out of love of G-d who commanded us to learn Torah.

The Gemara first mentions the two persons who learn for good reasons. They are the one who learns for the sake of the Torah and the one who learns for the sake of reward in the World to Come, for he will eventually come to learn *lishmah*, for the sake of Torah, in accord with a saying by Rav Yehudah: "By all means a person should engage in Torah study and good deeds even if he does not do it for its own sake, because by doing good for ulterior motives, one will eventually come to do good for its own sake" (Pesachim 50b).

This is the meaning of the Gemara: "Perform mitzvos for the sake of their maker," meaning to receive reward in the World to Come, in order that you will eventually come to do them *lishmah*, for the sake of the Torah, which is the highest level of doing a mitzvah.

Next the Gemara mentions the two persons who do the mitzvos for the wrong reasons, making the Torah a crown for self-glorification, or a spade with which to dig. About such persons the sages said, "One who makes use of the crown of Torah, will be uprooted from the world, and it would have been better had he not been created."

MESECHTA NAZIR

ANSWERING *AMEIN*

———=◈=———

NAZIR 66b

GEMARA: Rabbi Yose says: He who answers *"Amein"* does a greater mitzvah than he who re-cites the berachah.

T his statement has no connection with the topic of *nazir*, so why is it placed at the conclusion of *mesechta Nazir*?

The Rabbis tell us that the livelihood of a person is as difficult to provide as the Parting of the Red Sea (Pesachim 118a). Therefore, the Holy One, blessed be He, ordained that after one eats his fill he should say a berachah, as it says, *When you eat and are satisfied, you must bless Hashem your G-d* (*Devarim* 8:10). If one does so, G-d will bestow His blessing on him, giving him abundant food. Since sustenance is such a difficult thing, accusing angels try to deter G-d from giving ample sustenance. However, one's bera-chos come to one's defense, standing against the accusing angels. The berachos are like front-line soldiers, and the *amein* responses are like heroic fighters, doing battle against the accusers, the de-structive angels.

Now we understand how Rabbi Yose's statement relates to the Gemara. The last Mishnah in *Nazir* says that Shmuel and

Shimshon were *nazirim*. A *nazir* and a *parush* (ascetic) attaches himself to G-d, as it says, *He utters a nazirite's vow to set himself apart for Hashem* (*Bamidbar* 6:2) [By attaching himself to G-d, the *nazir*] is granted power and might to resist the accusing forces, as it says about Shimshon, *and he will begin to save Yisrael from the hands of the Philistines* (*Shofetim* 13:6). Under the leadership of Shmuel the Jews were also victorious in the wars against their enemies. [Just as a *nazir* is granted power over the accusing forces, so too, the berachos and *amein* responses one says, defend against the accusing heavenly forces.]

MESECHTA GITTIN

CHANNAH AND HER SEVEN SONS

———=◎=———

GITTIN 57a

GEMARA: *For Your sake we are killed all the time,*
we are considered as sheep for the slaughter
(*Tehillim* 44:23). Rabbi Yehudah says: This refers
to the woman [Channah] and her seven sons.
They brought the first son before the Emperor
[Antiochus Epiphanies] who said to him: Bow
down to the idol! He replied: It says in the Torah:
I am Hashem your G-d (*Shemos* 20:2). They led
him away and killed him. Then they brought the
second son to the Emperor who said to him: Bow
down to the idol! He replied: It says in the Torah:
Do not have any other gods before Me (*Shemos*
20:3). They led him away and killed him. They
brought in the third son and said to him: Bow
down to the idol! He replied: It says in the Torah:
Whoever sacrifices to any deity other than G-d, must
be condemned to death (*Shemos* 22:19). They led
him away and killed him. They brought in the
fourth son and said: Bow down to the idol! He
replied: It says in the Torah: *Do not bow down to*
any other god (*Shemos* 20:5). They led him away

and killed him. They brought in the fifth son and said: Bow down to the idol! He replied: It says in the Torah: *Listen, Yisrael, Hashem is our G-d; G-d is One* (*Devarim* 6:4). They led him away and killed him. They brought in the sixth son and said: Bow down to the idol! He replied: It says in the Torah: *Realize today and ponder in your heart: G-d is the Supreme Being in heaven above and on earth below—there is no other* (*Devarim* 4:39). They led him away and killed him. Finally they brought in the seventh son and said to him: Bow down to the idol! He replied: It says in the Torah: *Today you have declared allegiance to G-d . . . G-d has similarly declared allegiance to you* (*Devarim* 26:17,18).

The Emperor said to the seventh son: "I will throw down my seal before you, stoop down to pick it up, and people will say you conformed to the wish of the king." The child replied, "Shame on you Caesar! If your own honor is so important, how much more so is the honor of the Holy One, blessed be He!"

Why did each of the sons answer with a different verse, rather than all replying with the same verse? In fact, the second son's verse, *Do not have any other gods before Me,* is preceded immediately by the verse, *I am Hashem your G-d,* [which was said by the first son.] Additionally, the verses are not listed in the order in which they appear in the Torah. Finally: Why does the verse, *For Your sake we are killed all the time,* apply to these seven sons more than to all the other martyrs who gave their lives for the sanctification of G-d's Name?

Possibly, each of the seven sons was killed *al kiddush Hashem* on a different day of the week, and each quoted a verse relevant to the day on which he was killed.

When it says: "They brought the first" it means "on the first day of the week." He said: *I am Hashem your G-d*, because on the first day of Creation, the angels and heavenly bodies, which can mislead idolaters into ascribing divine powers to them, had not yet been created.

On the second day of the week the second son was executed. He said: *Do not have any other god before Me*, because on the second day of Creation, the angels, which may bring one to believe that G-d is composed of two beings, were created.

On the third day, active forces on earth were brought into being. The waters were gathered and the earth was told to send forth vegetation, both of which may lead to the idolatrous belief that there are godlike forces other than G-d on earth. Therefore the third son said: *Whoever sacrifices to any deity other than G-d must be condemned to death.*

On the fourth day, the luminaries and the constellations were created. We are commanded by the fourth son's verse, *Do not bow down to any other god*, not to attribute divine powers to them, as idolaters do, as it says, *When you raise your eyes to the sky, and see the sun, moon, and stars and other heaven bodies, do not bow down to them or worship them. It was to all the [other] nations under the heavens that Hashem made them a portion* (*Devarim* 4:19).

On the fifth day, creatures of the water and sky were created from the heaven and the earth, as it says, *The water shall teem with swarms of living creatures. Flying creatures shall fly over the land* (*Bereishis* 1:20). So that people should not believe a combined force from heaven and earth sustains these creatures, the fifth son said: *Realize today and ponder in your heart: G-d is the supreme Being in heaven above and on earth below—there is no other.*

On the sixth day animals and man were created. Lest people link G-d with man, the sixth son said, *Listen, Yisrael, Hashem is our G-d; G-d is One.*[9]

---

[9]   In our text the fifth son said *Listen Yisrael*, and the sixth said, *Realize today and ponder in your heart.*

To preclude the belief that after creating the world, G-d with-drew from the earth on the seventh day, no longer taking note of what people are doing, the seventh son said, *Today you have de-clared allegiance to G-d . . . G-d has similarly declared allegiance to you.* This proves that G-d [continuously] watches over us. In fact, the mitzvah of Shabbos attests to this, as it says, *It is a sign between Me and you* (*Shemos* 31:13), for we rest on Shabbos because He ceased from all the work of Creation.

The Gemara cites the verse, *For Your sake we are killed all the time, we are considered as sheep for the slaughter,* regarding [the tragic story of the martyrdom of Channah and her seven sons,] be-cause this entire chapter [in *Tehillim*] alludes to this incident. *The voice of the reviler and blasphemer, because of the enemy and avenger* (v.17) refers to the Emperor. *All this came upon us, yet we have not forgotten You, and we have not been false to Your covenant* (v.18), parallels the son's verse, *Do not have any other gods before Me.*

The psalm continues, *Our heart has not turned back* (v.19) to match the son's verse, *Whoever sacrifices to any deity other than G-d must be condemned to death.* Verse 19 continues, *nor have our foot-steps strayed from Your path*; this corresponds with *Do not bow down to any other god.* The next passage, *Have we forgotten the name of our G-d?* (v.21), is in accord with, *Listen, Yisrael, Hashem is our G-d; G-d is One.* The next passage, *Have we extended our hands to a strange god?* (v.21) is consistent with, *Realize today and ponder in your heart: G-d is the supreme Being in heaven above and on earth below—there is no other.*

The next verse, *Surely G-d can examine this, for he knows the secrets of the heart* (v.22) refers specifically to the Emperor's state-ment to the seventh son: "I will throw down my seal before you, so you can stoop to pick it up." The son replied: "Shame on you Caesar! If your own honor is so important, how much more is the honor of the Holy One, blessed be He!" The Emperor only desired that it appear as if he were worshipping the idol, though he did not believe in it. The son said, "Although it says, *Surely G-d can exam-ine this, for he knows the secrets of the heart,* meaning Hashem can discern if one does not believe in idols in his heart, still one should not bow to them because onlookers might think he is sincere.

The psalm concludes, *For Your sake we are killed all day long.* *All day long,* refers to being killed on each of the seven days of the week, and to the fact that the signs of the zodiac of each day are against us. The verse uses the plural, *For Your sake we are killed,* referring to the seven sons. The feminine form [katzon tivchah] is used in the verse, *We are considered as sheep for the slaughter,* because it refers to their mother.

MESECHTA SOTAH

Torah Study and Doing Mitzvos

————◆————

SOTAH 21a

GEMARA: The verse, *For the mitzvah is a candle, and the Torah is light* (*Mishlei* 6:23), compares a mitzvah to a candle, and Torah to light. Mitzvah is a candle, implies that just as a candle burns for a limited time only, so too, a mitzvah protects you only for a limited time. The Torah is compared to light, because just as light shines forever, so does learning Torah protect you forever.

It says, *When you walk, it will lead you, when you lie down, it will watch over you, and when you wake up, it will talk with you* (*Mishlei* 6:22). *When you walk it will lead you*—in this world, *when you lie down it will watch over you*—in death. *When you wake up, it will talk with you*—in the World to Come.

This may be illustrated with a parable: A person walking in darkness in the middle of the night is afraid of thorns, pits, thistles, wild beasts and robbers. Furthermore, he does not know the way. With a burning torch, he can be safe from thorns, pits and thistles, but wild beasts and robbers can

54

still harm him, and he does not know which way to go. When dawn breaks, he may be safe from wild beasts and robbers, but he still does not know which way to go. If he reaches a fork in the road [and reads the road sign] he can be completely safe. [The torch represents the mitzvos, the light of dawn symbolizes the Torah, and the fork in the road signifies the day of death.]

Rav Yosef says: A mitzvah protects you [from punishment] and saves you [from the *yetzer hara,* the evil impulse] as long as you are in the process of doing the mitzvah, but when you are no longer engaged in the mitzvah, it will protect you from punishment, but will not save you from the *yetzer hara.* However, the Torah you learned protects you [from punishment] and saves you [from the *yetzer hara*] whether you are busy studying it or not.

The verse, *When you walk, it will lead you, when you lie down it will watch over you, and when you wake up, it will talk with you* (*Mishlei* 6:22), refers to Torah study, which protects forever. Thus the sages expound: *When you walk it will lead you*—in this world, for in this world the Torah will lead you, relieving you from distress; *when you lie down it will watch over you*—in death, for when you lie in the grave, the Torah will guard against the agonies of the grave; *When you wake up it will talk with you*—in the World to Come, for in the World to Come, the Torah will speak up for you and defend you, shielding you from the judgment of Gehinnom.

Tosafos ask: If a mitzvah protects [you from punishment] even when you are not longer engaged in it, then a mitzvah also protects you forever. [If so, how is Torah study superior to doing a mitzvah?]

We can answer, that a mitzvah protects you forever in this world, whereas the Torah [you learned] protects you from the judgment of Gehinnom in the World to Come as well, as we derive from the verse, *and when you wake up, it will talk with you,* in the World to Come.

The Gemara then cites the parable of a man walking in darkness. On a deeper level this can be explained as follows: Man is a composite of body and soul. The body performs the act of the mitzvah, while the soul—man's intellect—fulfills the reasoning aspect [of the mitzvah], which is the Torah. There are three obstacles which stand in the way of attaining perfection [symbolized by the thorns, the pits and the thistles]. Just as the torch in the night saves a man from thorns, so do the mitzvos save him in this world from the tribulations that are related to this world, such as plague, war, and famine. The thorns symbolize famine and the difficulty of earning a livelihood; the pits represent plague, and the thistles symbolize the adversities of war. The mitzvah, which represent physical perfection protects man from these scourges.

But he must also overcome two obstacles which block his road to spiritual perfection. They are the *yetzer hara*, and bad friends who encourage him to stray, symbolized by the wild beasts and the robbers. The merit of the mitzvos he did, will not save him from these [spiritual] deterrents, because doing a mitzvah is a physical act. He is saved [from these two spiritual hindrances] only through the merit of his Torah learning, which is of a spiritual nature. Torah is the daybreak [in the parable] that saves him from the *yetzer hara* and bad friends.

THREE SETS OF STONES

———◦◉◦———

SOTAH 35b

GEMARA: From the episode [of the crossing of the Yarden] we can learn that there were three sets of stones. Moshe erected one set in the land of Moav, as it says, *In Transjordan, in the land of*

Moav, Moshe began to elucidate the Torah, and it says, *and you shall write on them [the stones] all the words of the Torah* . . . Yehoshua erected the second set in the middle of the Yarden . . . The third set was erected in Gilgal [by Yehoshua.]

Yehoshua took stones from the bed of the Yarden and erected them in Gilgal [as a remembrance for the splitting of the Yarden] as it says explicitly, *So that this will be a sign in your midst, when your children ask tomorrow: "[Of] what [significance] are these stones to you?" You shall tell them: "They signify that the waters of the Yarden were cut off before the Ark of the Covenant of Hashem . . . and these stones shall remain a remembrance for the children of Yisrael forever . . . and they remained there to this day* (*Yehoshua* 4:6,9).

What was the purpose of the stones Moshe erected? Why are they mentioned here, since they have no connection with the crossing of the Yarden under Yehoshua's leadership?

The purpose of the stones can be explained based on the teaching of the *Baal Ha'ikkarim*[10] who says, our faith is based on three fundamental principles: (1) The Torah was given by G-d. (2) G-d, who created the world out of nothing, exists. (3) G-d rewards man for his good deeds and punishes him for his evil deeds.

A stone symbolizes a fundamental doctrine, a cornerstone of faith, as it says, *He shepherded the stone of Yisrael* (*Bereishis* 49:24). The Gemara mentions three stones, to allude to these three fundamental principles.

The stones on which Moshe wrote the Torah, symbolize the principle that the Torah was brought down by him from Heaven.

The stones at Gilgal were used to build an altar on Mount Eival where the blessings and curses were pronounced (*Devarim* 7:11-26). The blessings and curses express the principle that G-d rewards good and punishes evil.

---

[10] A major work on Jewish philosophy and theology, by Rabbi Yosef Albo (1357-1445), the rabbi of Daroca and Soria in Spain.

The stones [Yehoshua] erected in the Yarden proclaim the
message that G-d exists and has the power to create the world out
of nothing, as can be seen by the fact that the waters of the Yarden
were cut off before the Holy Ark.

TWO VERSIONS OF G-D'S NAME

---◆---

SOTAH 40b

GEMARA: The Rabbis taught: How do we know
that *Amein* was not said in the *Beis Hamikdash?* It
says in response to a blessing in the *Beis
Hamikdash, Rise up and bless Hashem your G-d,
from this world to the World to Come!* (*Nechemiah*
9:5). How do we know that every berachah must
be followed by an expression of praise? It says, *Let
them bless Your glorious name which is exalted above
every blessing and praise* (ibid.) which means: For
every berachah give praise.

According to the Kabbalists, the word *amein,* which is an expression of affirmation and testimony, combines the name
of G-d as it is pronounced—א-ד-נ-י with the name as it is written—
י-ה-ו-ה. By adding the gematria of these two versions we obtain
91[11], which equals the gematria of *amein.* Outside the Beis
Hamikdash, where the divine name is pronounced as *A-D-N-Y,* it
was necessary to concentrate mentally on the written divine name
Y-H-V-H, this was achieved by answering *amein* whose gematria
equals these two Names. This is the underlying idea of the Gemara

---

[11] The gematria of A-D-N-Y is 1+4+50+10=65; the gematria of Y-H-V-H is
10+5+6+5=26; 65+26=91; the gematria of *amein is* 1+40+50=91.

in *Nazir* 66b: He who answers *amein* performs a greater mitzvah he who recites the berachah, because by saying *amein* he combines the written and the pronounced version of the divine name. *Amein* was not said in the Beis Hamikdash, because the divine Name was always pronounced there as it is written, and there is no combination adding up to the word *amein*. Instead, one says praise on every blessing, meaning that in a blessing in the Beis Hamikdash one always adds, *bless Hashem your G-d from this world to the World to Come;* and one responds to the blessing with the praise, *Blessed is the name of His glorious kingdom for all eternity!*

The verse, *bless Hashem your G-d from this world to the World to Come*, refers to the exalted name of G-d, *Y-H-V-H*, which is recited in the Beis Hamikdash now in this world as it will be recited in the World to Come. However outside the Beis Hamikdash, G-d's name is pronounced *A-D-N-Y*, until the days of the World to Come.

MESECHTA KIDDUSHIN

THREE CROWNS

GEMARA: King Yannai [a kohen from the Hasmonean dynasty] conquered sixty towns in the Kuchlit wilderness. On his return he invited the Sages [to a celebratory banquet], saying: "Our ancestors [who were very poor] ate *meluchim* [unappetizing herbs] when they built the [second] Beis Hamikdash. Let us also eat *meluchim* in memory of our ancestors, [and thank G-d for our prosperity]." They served *meluchim* on golden tables, and ate them. Elazar ben Po'irah, an evil-minded scoffer [of the *Tzedokim* (Sadducee) sect,] said to King Yannai: "O King Yannai! The hearts of the *Perushim* [Pharisees] are against you." King Yannai asked, "What shall I do [to prove that you are correct]?" Elazar ben Po'irah advised him to wear the headplate [of the Kohen Gadol on which the Divine Name is inscribed] on his forehead. With this act Yannai forced the sages to stand [since one must stand in honor of the Divine Name.] Yehudah ben Gedidiah, an elder sage, called out: "King Yannai, the crown of royalty is enough for you. Leave the crown of priesthood to the descendants of Aharon!"—for it was reported that Yannai's mother had been taken captive in Modi'in [and a son born to a woman after she was taken captive, is unfit to be a kohen].

Because the charge against his mother was investigated and proved to be unfounded, Yannai was incensed at the Sages of Yisrael. Elazar b. Po'irah incited King Yannai further: "O King Yannai! An ordinary Jew must tolerate such ridicule. But as king and Kohen Gadol, should you suffer such indignities?" Asked Yannai: "What shall I do?" Elazar b. Po'irah replied: "Kill them all!" Yannai exclaimed, "But what will become of the Torah [if all the Torah scholars are killed]?" Elazar b. Po'irah retorted: "[We don't need the Sages,] the Torah is wrapped and lying in the corner; whoever wants to study it can come and learn!" Said R. Nachman b. Yitzchak: At that point Yannai became a heretic, because he should have answered: "This applies to the Written Torah, [which is available for anyone to study,] but what about [Mishnah and Gemara,] the Oral Torah, [which can only be taught by Sages?]" Thus was evil immediately unleashed through Elazar ben Po'irah. All the Sages of Yisrael were killed, and the world was devoid of Torah, until Shimon ben Shetach arrived and restored the Torah to its original glory.

Yannai had acted as a legitimate kohen until now, performing the service in the Beis Hamikdash. Why hadn't Yehuda ben Gedidiah protested before this?

Additionally: What did Elazar B. Po'irah mean by saying, "The hearts of the *Perushim* [Pharisees] are against you"?

There are three crowns; the crown of Torah, the crown of *ke-hunah,* and the crown of kingship; but the crown of a good name surpasses them all (Avos 4:16). The crown of kingship is the crown that King David wore. The crown of *kehunah* refers to the head-plate [*tzitz*] of the Kohen Gadol, which resembled a crown. The crown of Torah alludes to the head-tefillin every Jew wears. In fact, the Torah word for tefillin, is *totefes,* which is used by the sages in reference to a crown.

The Name of Hashem is associated with all three crowns: The words *Kodesh LaShem* (sanctified to Hashem) were inscribed on the headplate of the Kohen Gadol. The tefillin are embossed with the letter *shin* of G-d's name *Shad-dai.* And in association with the royal crown it says, *Shlomoh sat upon the throne of Hashem (1 Divrei Hayamim* 29:23). Thus we can understand the Mishnah, "but the crown of a good Name [of Hashem] is on them all," in a literal sense.

After winning the war, King Yannai invited the Sages who were *Perushim*[12] to a banquet. They served unpalatable *meluchim* on golden tables, to indicate that in a moment of triumph one should remember one's days of poverty and wretchedness.

Elazar, as a member of the *Tzedokim,*[13] did not want to accept the doctrine of serving G-d without expecting a reward. Therefore, he incited the king [against the Sages] implying that they served *meluchim* to denigrate the importance of the banquet and humiliate Yannai by suggesting he was not worthy of the *kehunah* and the kingship.

By advising Yannai to wear the *tzitz* on his forehead, [he was actually telling him to remove his tefillin,] because the Gemara says there is only enough room on the head to lay two tefillin (Eruvin 95b). The Gemara derives this fact from the Kohen Gadol, who

---

[12] *Perushim* also known as Pharisees were the rabbis and devout Jews who strictly observed the Torah and the mitzvos.

[13] The *tzedokim,* also known as Sadducees were a heretical sect, who adhered to the Written Torah but repudiated the *Torah she'b'al peh,* the Oral Torah, rejecting the belief in *techiyas hameisim,* revival of the dead.

wore the tefillin in addition to his headplate. Were Yannai to v
the headplate together with the crown of kingship, he would pe
force have to remove the tefillin, since there is no room on the
head for all three crowns. Indeed it is impossible to be a king and
a kohen gadol, because both the king and the kohen gadol must
wear tefillin symbolizing their dedication to Torah, as it says
Through me, [the Torah,] kings will reign (*Mishlei* 8:15). Elazar, the
heretic, misled the king by telling him to put the headplate—the
crown of *kehunah*—on his head, knowing this would not be allowed because he was already wearing the crown of kingship.
Understanding this, Yehudah ben Gedidiah explained: "The crown
of royalty is enough for you. Leave the crown of priesthood to the
descendants of Aharon. If you don't, you will dislodge the tefillin—the crown of Torah; for it is impossible to wear three crowns
on your head at the same time, and you need the crown of Torah."

The heretical group maliciously twisted Yehudah ben
Gedidiah's words, saying he meant to malign Yannai and imply that
he was unfit to be Kohen Gadol since his mother was taken captive.

Elazar told Yannai that the Torah is wrapped up and lying in
the corner, whoever wants to study it can come and learn! He was
telling him not to be concerned with removing the crown of Torah
from himself, because others can wear the crown of Torah. This
was also misleading, because the king also needs the crown of
Torah.

The world was devoid of Torah, until Shimon ben Shetach
came and restored the Torah to its original glory, demonstrating
that the king needs the crown of Torah and it cannot be pushed
aside by the two crowns of kingship and *kehunah*.

The Sages protested [when Yannai put on the *tzitz*,] since with
this action he displaced the tefillin, the crown of Torah, in favor of
the two other crowns. However they did not object when he performed the service in the Beis Hamikdash despite the rumor about
his mother, because even were the rumor true, the service of a
kohen who is unfit, is acceptable ex post facto, after it had been
done.

TWO FORMS OF THE DIVINE NAME

KIDDUSHIN 71a

GEMARA: Rabbi Avina explains: It says, *This is My name forever . . . . and this is how I am to be remembered for all generations* (*Shemos* 3:15). The Holy One, blessed be He, said: I am not called as I am written. I am written with *yud-hei*, but I am read, *alef dalet*. [The Divine Four-Letter name is *yud-hei-vav-hei,* but it is read *alef-dalet-nun-yud*].

The Rabbis said (Pesachim 50b): In this world G-d's name is pronounced A-D-N-Y, but in the World to Come, He is called as He is written, Y-H-V-H. During Creation, G-d merged the Attributes of Mercy and Justice, as it says, . . . *on the day that Hashem Elokim made earth and heaven* (*Bereishis* 2:4), [and we know that the Name Hashem denotes the Attribute of Mercy, and the Name Elokim represents the attribute of Justice.] The written form of the Name, Y-H-V-H, represents the attribute of Mercy, and the pronounced form of the Name, A-D-N-Y, represents the attribute of Justice. Since, the World to Come is dominated completely by Mercy, in time to come, G-d's Name will be whole, and the pronounced version will be identical to the written version. In this world, He is called A-D-N-Y, which is a form of remembrance, and remembrance suggests judgment. Indeed Rosh Hashanah, the Day of Judgment, is called the Day of Remembrance. The Name A-D-N-Y [*alef, dalet, nun, yud*] alludes to this. The *alef,* which is numerically equal to one, alludes to Rosh Hashanah [the first day of the year], and the *yud,* which is numerically equal to ten, alludes to *Yom Kippur* [the 10th of *Tishrei*]. Situated between the *alef* and the *yud* are the letters *dalet, nun,* which form the word *dan,* "to judge," because the ten days between Rosh Hashanah and Yom Kippur are days of judgment.

In the World to Come, which will be ruled entirely by Mercy, G-d's name will be read in the form of Mercy. In fact even in this world, when mentioning G-d's name in one's prayers, one should have in mind His attribute of Mercy, which is manifest in its written form, for the written form of words have significance.

This is the underlying thought of the verse, *Seek Hashem as He is be found, call upon Him when He is near* (*Yeshayah* 55:6). *Seek Hashem*—mentally in your heart, *as He is found,* meaning the way his Name is written, but, *call upon Him,* meaning, although it is to be vocalized differently, *when He is near,* do it in a manner that is close to the way it is written, because the vowel marks [*sh'va, cholam, kametz*] are identical in the written and pronounced forms of the Name.

MESECHTA BAVA KAMMA

EISAV, THE ROOT OF CALAMITY

BAVA KAMMA 3b

GEMARA: "There are four categories of damages: the ox, the pit, the *mav'eh*, and the fire."

The Gemara asks: What is *mav'eh*? Rav says: *mav'eh* is a man [who causes damage]. [The word *be'ayu* which has the same root as *mav'eh* is used in reference to man] as it says, *He calls out to Me because of Se'ir. "Watchman, what of the night [of exile]? The Watchman says: "Morning is coming [for the righteous], but also night [for the wicked].* Im tevayun be'ayu—*If you really pray for it, repent and it will come (Yeshayah 21:12).*

Shmuel said: *Mav'eh* means "tooth"—[damage caused by livestock grazing in another person's field. The word *niv'u* is related to the word *mav'eh*, which means, "revealed" and it refers to the teeth of an animal, which are normally hidden, but become revealed in grazing.] As it says, *How has Eisav been searched, his hoards revealed [niv'u]? (Ovadiah 1:6).*

66

This calls for an explanation. Because Rav finds the word *be'ayu* used in connection with man, should we use the term *mav'eh* for man when he does damage? And because Shmuel finds the word *niv'u*, used in relationship to a tooth, should we term the grazing of livestock as *mav'eh*? Why not use the common terms *man* and *tooth* instead of the farfetched word *mav'eh*?

We may explain this based on the following: There are four primary categories of disaster. Three of them, pestilence, sword (war), and famine, are mentioned in the verse, . . . *for war, for evil, and for pestilence* (*Yirmeyah* 28:8). One may escape from these scourges with help from G-d. However [the fourth calamity], that of blazing fire is worse, for it causes total devastation [and no one escapes]. About [the curse of fire] it says, *Had not Hashem, Master of Legions, left us a trace of a remnant, we would have been like Sedom, we would have resembled Amorah* (*Yeshayah* 1:9), for Sedom was punished by fire and totally wiped out, as it says, *Hashem made sulfur and fire rain down on Sedom and Amorah—it came from Hashem. He overturned these cities along with the entire plain* [destroying everyone who lived there] (*Bereishis* 18:24).

This Mishnah, the first in the tractate, lists the four categories of damages, for which one must make monetary compensation, corresponding to the four major catastrophes brought on by Heaven.

The ox corresponds to the bane of famine, as it says, *Many crops come [through] the power of the ox* (*Mishlei* 14:4), and the ox includes damage to the crops which come about through the tooth and the foot of an animal.

The pit alludes to death by pestilence, as it says [referring to one who was sick, *Hashem my G-d, I have prayed to You and You have healed me. . .] You have preserved me from my descent to the pit* (*Tehillim* 30:4).

Mav'eh, whether it is interpreted as damage done by man, or damage done by the tooth, corresponds to [the ravages of war caused by Eisav.] If we interpret *mav'eh* as man, [which in Hebrew is *adam*], it relates to Eisav, [who is also called *Edom*], as it says, *I put* adam *in your place and nations in place of your soul* (*Yeshayah* 43:4). This verse can also be read, *I put Edom in your place.*

If we interpret *mav'eh* as the damage of the tooth, it is similar to the sword, which corresponds to the ravages of war and the power of Eisav about whom it says, *You shall live by your sword* (*Bereishis* 27:40).

Both Rav and Shmuel agree that we are dealing about damage corresponding to Eisav; because they did not want to mention this openly, they called it *mav'eh* which is used in verses pertaining to Eisav.

Rav says *mav'eh* refers to damage done by man, quoting a verse about Eisav, *He calls to Me because of Se'ir* [who is Eisav]. This refers to [our present-day] exile of Edom, which exemplifies the power of the sword. The verse continues, *If you really pray*—to be saved from this exile—*repent and come,* for with prayer and supplication you will be saved from the hand of Eisav, as it says, *[When] the voice [of prayer and Torah] is Yaakov's voice, [he will be saved from] the hands that are the hands of Eisav* (*Bereishis* 27:22). Thus man is called *mav'eh*—one who prays.

According to Shmuel, *mav'eh* denotes [damage caused by] the tooth. This alludes to Eisav who is compared to a wild boar whose strength is in its teeth. Daniel alludes to this in his vision of the fourth beast, *which was exceedingly terrifying with teeth of iron and claws of copper; it devoured and crumbled, and trampled what remained with its feet* (*Daniel* 7:19). [Eisav, The wild boar,] will overpower all nations, destroying them with its teeth. Since the boar does not chew its cud, its teeth imply that it is a non-kosher animal and therefore does not have power over Yisrael. The boar will only be able to overcome Yisrael with its feet, which have split hooves and are a sign of purity.[14] The verse, *with teeth of iron and claws of copper it devoured and crumbled, and trampled what remained with its feet,* means Eisav was able to attack all the other nations with its teeth and they were devoured and crumbled, however that which

---

[14] An animal may be eaten only if it has split hooves and brings up its cud (*Vayikra* 11:3).

remained, referring to Yisrael, as they are called *the remnants of Yisrael*, will only be trampled with the kosher feet. This is the meaning of the verse referring to Eisav, *Blessed is Hashem, who did not present us as prey for their teeth* (*Tehillim* 124:6), for He did not subjugate Yisrael to the non-kosher teeth of Eisav. Accordingly, Shmuel interprets the verse referring to Eisav, which says, *his hidden things were revealed*, to mean, his teeth which are usually hidden, have been exposed, and will not be capable of harming Yisrael.

The Mishnah lists fire as the last type of damage caused by man. It corresponds to destruction by fire, and is called *he'evar*, which means consumption because it consumes everything in its path. May G-d protect us from these four catastrophes.

GUIDELINES FOR PIETY

BAVA KAMMA 30a

GEMARA: Rav Yehudah said: If a person wants to be pious [a *chassid*] he should be especially careful in observing the laws [that are discussed in] the order of *Nezikin* [which deal with monetary matters and financial disputes]. Rava said: He should observe the ethical guidelines of *mesechta Avos*. Others say: He should concentrate on [matters that are discussed] in *mesechta Berachos*, [namely, the various berachos that should be recited].

I t seems to me that a *chassid* is one who acts in the best manner possible. Rabbi Pinchas ben Ya'ir enumerates ten [commendable] qualities, saying: Torah study brings you to caution, caution to enthusiasm, enthusiasm to innocence, innocence to abstinence, abstinence to purity . . . *Chassidus* (piety) is listed as the supreme quality, "for *chassidus* brings you to [the possession of] *ruach hakodesh* [the holy spirit]" (Avodah Zarah 20b).

Man's good deeds fall into three categories: Deeds that are good towards Heaven, good towards his fellowman, or towards himself.

Rav Yehudah, addressing how one should be good to his fellowman, cautioned people to be especially careful with the laws [of monetary matters and business disputes discussed in] the order of *Nezikin*.

Rava, addressing how one should be good towards himself, stressed the observance of the rules of ethics in *mesechta Avos*.

Others, addressing how one should be good towards heaven, emphasized concentration on [matters discussed] in *mesechta Berachos* [namely, the various berachos one should recite].

GREETING QUEEN SHABBOS

BAVA KAMMA 32a

> GEMARA: Rabbi Chanina [went to the field to wel-come Shabbos, saying,] "Come let us go forward to greet the bride, the queen!" Rabbi Yannai wrapped himself [in his Shabbos attire], and re-mained in his place saying, "Enter, O bride! Enter, O bride!"

The rabbis addressed Shabbos as "bride" based on this Midrash: [When Adam named every animal and bird he complained:] "For each of these, there is a mate, yet for me there is no mate." Answered G-d: "Shabbos shall be your mate." And in-deed on the seventh day, Shabbos is married to Yisrael. At twilight on Friday, the Shabbos is like a bride entering the *chuppah* canopy.

Just as a bride is married through *kiddushin* [the marriage service], so does the Shabbos become married to Yisrael through the *Kiddush* on Friday night. The Shabbos is called "queen" because all Jews are princes. Rabbi Chanina said: "Let us go forward to greet the bride," because it is customary for a *chassan* to walk forward to greet the *kallah*.

Rabbi Yannai remained standing and said, "Enter, O bride! Enter, O bride!" implying that the *kallah* should come to him, like a bride who leaves her father's house after the wedding to enter her husband's home. The invitation is repeated as if to say: "Enter, O *kallah* under the *chuppah!* Enter, O *kallah* into your husband's house!"

AWE FOR TORAH SCHOLARS

BAVA KAMMA 41b

GEMARA: Wherever the word *es*, [which is used as a direct object] occurred in the Torah, Shimon Ha'emsoni expounded on the word adding to the subject matter at hand. He did not expound the verse, *You shall fear es Hashem your G-d* (*Devarim* 6:13) [because he was reluctant to say that anything should be venerated like G-d]. His students questioned him: "Rabbi, what will be with all the *es*'s that you expounded?" He replied: "Just as I was rewarded for the exposition [*derishah*], so will I be rewarded for discontinuing [*perishah*]." Later Rabbi Akiva came and taught: *You shall fear es Hashem you G-d*, means one should also revere *talmidei chachamim* (Torah scholars).

Rashi explains that Shimon Ha'emsoni was afraid to associate anyone or anything with the fear of G-d. From the verse itself, *You shall fear Hashem your G-d,* he inferred not to compare anything else with the fear of G-d. Therefore he said, "Just as I would have been rewarded for expounding this verse, by adding to the fulfillment of the mitzvah of fearing G-d, so too, will I be rewarded for not expounding this verse, because thereby I am also fulfilling the mitzvah of fearing G-d."

Rabbi Akivah felt that including Torah scholars in this verse, does not equate them with G-d; rather the awe one has for Torah scholars is in itself awe of G-d, for one who is in awe of Torah scholars will listen to them [when they tell him] to fear G-d and keep His mitzvos. Thus it says: "Let the reverence for your teacher be as the reverence of Heaven" (Avos 4:15), for revering one's teacher is in and of itself reverence of Heaven.

THE STRUCTURE OF *MEGILLAS EICHAH*

⟫⟫⟩◉⟨⟪⟪

BAVA KAMMA 55a

GEMARA: Rabbi Yehoshua said: If someone sees the letter *tes* in a dream it is a good omen. Is this because tes is the first letter of the word *tov,* "good"? Yet, *tes* is also the first letter of the word *Teteisiha,* which is used in the verse, *I will sweep it clean with the broom of destruction (Yeshayah* 14:23)? However [*teteisiha* has two *tes*'s] and he only saw one *tes* in his dream. But the *tes* can refer to the word *tumah* (defilement), as in, *Her impurity* [tum'asah] *is on her hems (Eichah* 1:9)? We must be dealing with one who saw in this dream, both a *tes* and a *beis.* Though one might think this can refer to the word *tav'u*, which has a *tes* and a *beis*, and means sunk, as in, *Her gates have sunk into the earth* (*Eichah* 2:9), we say *tes* is a good omen because the first time the letter *tes* occurs in the Torah, is in the word *tov*—good. From the first verse of *Bereishis* until the verse, *G-d saw that the light was good* (tov), no *tes* occurs.

Why did the Gemara say that one tes cannot refer to *tetisiha*, which has two *tes'*, but must refer to *tov*, or, *tumah*, which only begin with a *tes*? After all *tetisiha*, also begins with a *tes!* Additionally, if one sees a vision of the letters *tes* and *beis*, it seems obvious that he was shown the word *tov*, [for the two letters t-v spell the entire word *tov*, "good"]. Why should one think these letters refer to the word *tav'u* in which the letters *tes* and *beis* do not spell the whole word?

King Yehoyakim burned three chapters of *Megillas Eichah*, which are arranged according to the *alef-beis*. They are: *Eichah yashevah* "Alas — she sits in solitude" (ch.1), *Eichah ya'iv* "Alas—the L-rd in His anger has clouded" (ch.2), and *Eichah yu'am* "Alas—the gold is dimmed!" (ch.4). Yirmeyah added the chapter of *Ani hagever*—"I am the man who has seen affliction" (ch.3), which contains a triplicate of the *alef-beis*, corresponding to the three alefbeis' which were burnt. Why did Yirmeyah insert the new chapter *Ani Hagever* (ch.3) between chapters two and four, which were written earlier?

[The numeric value of *tes* is nine.] Because of our sins, the Beis Hamikdash was destroyed twice. Both destructions occurred on the ninth of Av; when the "sublime goodness", the *beis hamikdash* which is called the *hahar hatov*, "the good mountain" was taken from us. In the first two chapters of *Eichah* the letter *tes*, which symbolizes *tov*, "good," was changed to *ra*, "evil." In the first chapter the verse beginning with *tes*, says, *Her impurity* (tum'asah) *is on her hems* (1:9); and in the second chapter the verse beginning with *tes* says, *Her gates have sunk* (tav'u) *into the earth* (2:9). These verses allude to the two destructions that occurred on the ninth of Av, and correspond to the two *Luchos* (Tablets) that were shattered.

But lest one despair and say: There is no more *tov*—good—for Yisrael, G-d forbid, the *tes* in the [fourth chapter], which was originally the third chapter begins with the word *Tovim*—they were good. This chapter [alludes to the third Beis Hamikdash, and therefore] ends with the Redemption, saying, *Your iniquity is expiated, O daughter of Tzion. He will not exile you again* (4:22), an indication that after the two destructions the *tes* will never be changed [to evil] again. Rather, [the *tes* will remain] *for our good* [tov] *all the days [to come], to keep us alive as this very day* (*Devarim* 6:25). The ninth day of Av will become a day of joy and gladness with the rebuilding of the "good mountain."

King Yehoyakim burned the three chapters, which included the *tes* of the last chapter, which begins *Tovim*—They were good. Lest one say that by doing so he brought the goodness mentioned in that chapter to an end, Yirmeyah added the chapter *Ani Hagever*—"*I am the man who has seen affliction.*" In this chapter, each of the three verses that begin with *tes,* begin with the word tov—good, as a heartening message. [Yirmeyah wished to indicate] that Yisrael should be good toward G-d, good toward their fellowmen, and good towards themselves. Yirmeyah placed his chapter after the first two, which allude to the destruction and before the last one, which announces that the good will not change, and that evil will not befall us again.

Now we can understand the Gemara: Why doesn't *tes* refer to the first letter of *teteisiha, I will sweep it clean with the broom of destruction?* Because the Gemara knew the *tes* he saw refers to one of the verses of *Eichah*, not an acronym for any word beginning with *tes.* Thus they said *tes* refers to *tov*—good—which is the good and hopeful message of the fourth chapter. The Gemara then asks: Perhaps the *tes* alludes to the word *tumasa* of the first chapter, which refers to the destruction of the first *beis hamikdash?* Answers the Gemara: He was shown a *tes* and a *beis,* which form the word *tov.* Can the *tes-beis* refer to the word *tave'u* ["they have sunk"], which is the *tes* of the second chapter and refers to the second destruction? The Gemara answers that he saw only one *tes,* however, since the first *tes* in the Torah begins the word *tov*, we can be sure this dream shows a *tes* to represent the *tov*—good—mentioned in the fourth chapter, which tells us that the *tov* will never again be changed to bad.

G-D'S COMPENSATION

———◦◉◦———

BAVA KAMMA 60b

GEMARA: It says, *If a fire gets out of control and spreads through thorns* (*Shemos* 22:5). The phrase *gets out of control* implies [that the fire started] by itself, nevertheless, [the verse continues,] *the one who started it must make restitution.* [Metaphorically this is explained: Although Hashem didn't actually start the fire,] The Holy One, blessed be He, said: I will make restitution for the fire that I started. It was I who kindled the fire in Tzion, for it says, *He kindled a fire in Tzion which consumed its foundations* (*Eichah* 4:11). And in time to come, I will build Tzion up by fire, as it says, *And I will be for it a wall of fire all around, and for glory will I be in its midst* (*Zechariah* 2:9).

Bad things do not stem from G-d, for He is the ultimate good, having no connection to evil. Sin is the cause of evil, for when sin abounds it causes the *Shechinah* and G-d's benevolence to depart, allowing evil to occur. Thus it says, *If fire gets out of control*—by itself—because evil does not emanate directly from G-d. However in regards to good, such as paying for the damage, G-d says: "I am the One who set the fire," meaning, He will make restitution as if He actually set the fire.

MESECHTA BAVA METZIAH

THE TORAH IS NOT IN HEAVEN

———◆———

BAVA METZIAH 59b

GEMARA: We learned in a Mishnah: According to
Rabbi Eliezer, an oven built out of pottery sections, with a layer of sand between each section is
not susceptible to *tumah*. The Sages disagreed
saying, such an oven is susceptible to *tumah*. This
oven is called "the oven of Achna'i." Why was it
called "the oven of Achna'i"? Rabbi Yehudah said:
Because the Sages encircled the problem of this
oven with various proofs like an *achna'i*, [a snake
that coils itself], proving that it is susceptible to
tumah.

   On that day [when the vote was taken], Rabbi
Eliezer advanced every conceivable argument, but
the other Sages would not accept them. Rabbi
Eliezer said: "If the halachah is like me, let the
carob tree prove it!" The carob tree uprooted itself and moved a hundred cubits. Some say it
moved four hundred cubits from its place. The
Sages said: "You cannot bring proof from a carob
tree." Rabbi Eliezer said to them: "If the halachah
is like me, let the stream of water prove it!" The

water in the stream began flowing backward. The sages retorted: "You cannot bring proof from a stream of water!" Rabbi Eliezer persisted: "If the halachah agrees with me, let the walls of the *beis midrash* prove it!" Thereupon the walls began to tilt as if to fall. At this point Rabbi Yehoshua scolded the walls, saying: "When Torah scholars are involved in an halachic argument, what right have you to interfere?" Out of respect for Rabbi Yehoshua the walls did not collapse, and out of respect for Rabbi Eliezer they did not straighten up, remaining in their tilted position till this day. Finally Rabbi Eliezer said: "If the halachah agrees with me, let the heavens prove it!" Thereupon a heavenly voice was heard saying: "How can you argue with Rabbi Eliezer? The halachah is as he states in every instance!" But Rabbi Yehudah stood up and exclaimed: "[*The Torah*] *is not in heaven!*" (*Devarim* 30:12). What did Rabbi Yehudah mean by this? Rabbi Yirmeyah explains: Since the Torah has already been given to us at Mount Sinai, we do not pay attention to heavenly voices, because You have written, *A case must be decided on the basis of the majority* (*Shemos* 23:2).

Rabbi Nassan met Eliyahu and asked him, "What was the Holy One, blessed be He, doing at that time?" Eliyahu replied, "He was laughing with joy, and saying, 'My sons have defeated Me, My sons have defeated Me.'"

We can explain this Gemara in accordance with the Gemara in *Chagigah* (3b) which expounds the verse, *The words of the wise are like goads; and like well planted nails, are the sayings of the masters of assemblies, all coming from one Shepherd* (*Koheles* 12:11). The words of Torah are *well planted,* for just as a plant grows and spreads, so do the words of Torah grow and spread. *Masters of assemblies,* refer to Torah scholars who sit in numerous assemblies, occupying themselves with the Torah. Some declare a thing unclean while others pronounce it clean; some prohibit a thing while others permit it; some declare [a person] unfit [to be a witness or a kohen], while others declare him fit. [In view of the contradictory opinions of the rabbis,] a person might say: "This being so, how can I learn Torah?" Therefore it says, *all coming from one Shepherd.* One G-d gave them, one leader [Moshe] uttered them from the mouth of the Master of all creation. So too, make your ear like a funnel and make your heart perceptive to understand the words of those who pronounce clean and those who pronounce unclean . . . The words of those that pronounce clean and those that pronounce unclean, are all the words of the Living G-d, for valid arguments can be posited for both positions. However, the Torah was given to man on earth who must decide on the basis of the majority opinion, as it says, *A case must be decided on the basis of the majority.* Therefore, the Gemara says: Have a perceptive heart to understand, for a person should not reach a conclusion without carefully considering the matter before making a decision. That is why Rabbi Eliezer said to the rabbis: "True, you are in the majority. But when the Torah says, *Follow the majority,* it stipulated that [the majority opinion] should be *well planted;* just as a plant grows and increases, so do the words of Torah grow and increase. One must have a perceptive heart, which grows and develops in wisdom. But your ruling in opposition to my opinion, is like a carob that bears fruit only in once in seventy years. Your words are as barren as a carob which produces very little fruit."

The rabbis answered: "You cannot bring proof from a carob tree. Perhaps its lack of fruit tells us that you are in the minority, short on wisdom and knowledge."

Rabbi Eliezer then said: "Let the stream of water prove it!" He meant to imply that a majority of Sages agreed with his opinion, however, driven by pride, they were ashamed to take back what they had originally thought. He was hinting to the saying of the sages: Why are the words of the Torah compared to water? Just as water flows from a higher level to a lower level, so do the words of the Torah endure only with a person who is humble (Taanis 7a). Therefore he said: "Let the stream of water prove it!" Water usually flows in the way of the Torah from a high to a low level, but this stream will reverse itself, flowing from a lower to a higher level, just as you, because of your pride, are reversing the way of the Torah."

They answered: "You cannot bring proof from the stream of water! Perhaps it reversed its flow to demonstrate that you should not be followed and your reasoning is out of step, like the stream running backward!"

Rabbi Eliezer shot back: "Let the walls of the *beis midrash* prove it!" Everyone knows that a *beis midrash* is essential for Torah study. He insinuated: Your opposition to my opinion is just harassment; you are not sincere. With your [harmful] attitude toward Torah study, there is no need for a *beis midrash;* this *beis midrash* might as well collapse. Rabbi Yehoshua responded, "When Torah scholars are involved in an halachic argument, what right have you to interfere?" He meant to say that the walls cannot judge the sincerity of the sages, and the final *halachah* is based on the opinion of the rabbis. The *beis midrash* exists to learn Torah and the cases are decided according to the majority. Perhaps the wall remained tilted, to signify that in every generation there are scholars who learn for the sake of winning an argument and provoking their opponent, as indeed Rabbi Eliezer thought of the other rabbis, but others learn in order that the truth may emerge.

Rabbi Yehudah said: "[The Torah] is not in heaven! We do not pay attention to heavenly voices," because in fact, the Torah law is based on the opinion of the majority in this world.

G-d said: "My sons have defeated Me, My sons have defeated Me." The repetition of the phrase indicated that the sages on both sides, those that declared the oven unclean and those that declared it clean, had legitimate grounds for their view.

MESECHTA BAVA BASRA

LEARNING TORAH LATE AT NIGHT

━━━◍━━━

BAVA BASRA 10a

GEMARA: What does the phrase, *Upon awakening I will be sated by Your image* (*Tehillim* 17:15), mean? Rav Nachman bar Yitzchak says, *upon awakening* refers to Torah scholars who shun sleep from their eyes in this world [learning Torah late into the night]. The Holy One, blessed be He, will reward them by satiating them with the splendor of the *Shechinah.*

The Gemara in *Kiddushin* (82b) explains the verse, *Those who hope in Hashem will have renewed strength* (*Yeshayah* 40:31), to mean that the Torah imparts strength to a Torah scholar. Although one who is sleep deprived becomes weakened, G-d will grant strength to a Torah scholar who fights sleep to learn Torah, satiating him with the splendor of the *Shechinah* even in this world. This verse does not refer to the World to Come, where sleep and fatigue do not exist and the righteous continuously delight in the radiance of the *Shechinah.*

80

REWARD IN THIS WORLD AND THE NEXT

BAVA BASRA 15b

GEMARA: There was a righteous gentile named Iyov, who came to this world so that G-d would repay him in this world [for the good he did]. G-d gave him suffering and he began cursing and blaspheming. G-d then doubled his reward in this world, so he would be denied access to the World to Come.

Arighteous Jew knows his reward for serving G-d will not be given in this transitory world [but rather in the World to Come]. The Sages expound on the verse, *You shall observe the commandments . . . that I command you today* (*Devarim* 7:11)— *Today* you must do the mitzvos, and "tomorrow"—[the World to Come]—is reserved for receiving reward (*Eiruvin* 22a). This is not so with non-Jews, as it says, *He pays back His enemies in their lifetime* (*Devarim* 7:10). [G-d rewards them in this world for their good deeds, thus denying them the delights of the World to Come]. Although Scripture affirms, *that there is no one like him [Iyov] on earth, a wholesome and upright man* (*Iyov* 2:10), he was not a Jewish tzaddik, but a non-Jewish righteous man, who came to life to be rewarded in this world [for his good deeds]. If one thinks this is unfair, consider this: G-d afflicts a *tzaddik* in this world in order to erase his transgressions, [and the *tzaddik*] does not criticize G-d. Thus, Avraham was put to the test with ten trials and he never questioned G-d's ways. However, when G-d tormented Iyov in this world to cancel his sins and reward him abundantly in the World to Come, he reacted by berating G-d and criticizing His ways. Therefore, G-d doubled his reward in this world, paying him in full for his good deeds, and effectively shutting him out of the World to Come.

This is similar to the Gemara in *Chagigah*: Both a tzaddik and a *rasha* (wicked man), have two shares—one in Gan Eden and one in Gehinnom. When the tzaddik is deserving, he receives his share and the share of the *rasha* in Gan Eden. If the *rasha* is guilty, he receives his share and the share of the *tzaddik* in Gehinnom. However, the Holy One, blessed be He, does not withhold the reward of the *rasha* [for his good deeds]; He doubles his reward in this world, by giving him the portion of the *tzaddik* in this world.

THE AMAZING VOYAGES OF RABBAH BAR BAR CHANAH

———◈———

BAVA BASRA 73a

[The tales of Rabbah bar Bar Chanah, are among the most profound *aggados* in the Talmud.]

GEMARA: Rabbah [bar Bar Chanah] said: Sailors told me: The wave that sinks a ship seems to have a white fringe of fire at its crest. If you strike it with a club engraved with, *I am who I am* (*Shemos* 3:14), *Kah, the Lord of Hosts, amein, amein, selah*, it begins to subside.

Rabbah continued. Sailors told me: There are three hundred *parsah*[15] between one wave and the next, and the height of each wave is also three hundred *parsah*.

---

[15] A parsah is about 2½ miles.

There are elements [in this story that cannot be taken literally.] What is meant by the white fringe of fire [on the crest of the wave?] How does striking the wave with various Names of G-d cause it to subside? What is the significance of the three hundred *parsah* between each wave?

This can be explained based on a Gemara. Rabbi Akiva [said, "I was drowning.] Finding a plank from a ship, [I held on to it] and inclined my head in the direction of each wave that rolled over me." From this the Sages learned, that should bandits attack you, bend your head toward them [complying with their demands] *Yevamos* (121a).

One may wonder: What is the connection [between waves and bandits]? The answer is found in the verse, *All Your breakers and Your waves passed over me* (*Yonah* 2:4). The waves of the sea symbolize our afflictions and exile at the hands of wicked men. The *Midrash Yelamdeinu* says: Yisrael is compared to sand, as it says, *The number of the children of Yisrael will be like the sand of the sea that can neither be measured nor counted* (*Hoshea* 2:1). The nations of the world are compared to the sea, as it says, *Woe to the tumult of many nations, who are as tumultuous as the tumult of the seas* (*Yeshayah* 17:12). They hatch plots against Yisrael, but G-d makes them come to naught. Therefore Yeshayah says, *The wicked will be like the driven sea that cannot rest* (*Yeshayah* 57:20). Just as waves [do not learn from one another, so too, the wicked do not learn from their predecessors.] The first wave says: "I will flood the whole world!" but when it hits the sand it is forced to surrender. The next wave does not learn from the first [but tries to flood the world, and is defeated]. Similarly, Pharaoh oppressed Yisrael, but G-d crushed him. Amalek and Sichon did not learn a lesson from him.

The Sages learned to deal with a bandit from a wave, advising us to bow our head, yielding to him. Rabbah bar Bar Chanah had this in mind when he said: "Sailors told me." The "sailors" are the Jewish people who navigate the sea of the exile like a ship adrift in the blustery sea, tossed by the surging waves. [The waves stand for] the evildoers of every generation who try to sink the ship—Yisrael.

The fiery crest on the wave represents the Guardian Angel of the nations who try to destroy us. We must strike them with a club engraved with the words, *I am who I am,* for this is the Name Hashem revealed to Moshe at the Burning Bush, telling him, "Just as I am with them in this exile so will I be with them to protect them in future exiles." The word, *Kah,* is a Name of Hashem associated with exile, as Hashem said *My hand is on the throne of Kah,* from where our sages derive that the Name of Hashem will not be complete until the future. *The Lord of Hosts,* is the Name by which we will be redeemed, as it says, *Redeem us, the Lord of Hosts* (*Yeshayah* 47:4). *Amein,* means faith, and through faith we will merit redemption. The second *amein* refers to the merit of saying, *Amein Yehei Shemei Rabbah* in the Kaddish prayer.

Rabbah bar Bar Chanah said there are three hundred *parsah* between one wave and the next, referring to the time between one era of persecution and the next. Each oppressor was empowered by his sign of the zodiac. Each sign of the zodiac reigns for thirty days in which an average person can walk 300 *parsah*[16]. Our first exile was under Pharaoh who was represented by the constellation of the Ram (Aries), and the second exile was under Nevuchadnetzar [king of Babylonia] whose constellation was Lion (Leo).

THE SLAYING OF THE YETZER HARA

———◈———

BAVA BASRA 73a,b

GEMARA: Rabbah bar Bar Chanah further said: I saw [the demon] Hurmin, son of Lilis, running along the battlements of the walls of Mechuzah. A rider galloping below on horseback could not catch up with him. Once two mules were saddled

---

16 An average person can walk ten parsah per day.

for Hurmin, standing on two bridges across the Donag River. He jumped back and forth from one to the other, holding two glasses of wine in his hands, pouring wine from one into the other without spilling a drop. This happened on a day that was so stormy that *those who go down into the sea in ships rise heavenward and descend to the depths* (*Tehillim* 107:26). When the king's agents heard about Hurmin's juggling stunt they killed him.

Rashbam explains that this story shows G-d's mercy on people, not allowing these [demons] to harm them. This explanation is questionable, because if that is the message, the entire story is unnecessary.

Our sages say Satan is both the *yetzer hara* (evil impulse), and the Angel of Death. He descends [to earth] tempting people to sin, and after they sin he rises [to Heaven] to denounce them. Then he descends again to grab their soul. Hurmin is one of Satan's troops. He chooses the most outstanding individuals as his victims, as the saying goes: The greater the man, the stronger is his *yetzer hara* (Sukkah 52a). Thus, he focuses primarily on the people of Yisrael, to entice them. This is the meaning of "he was running along the battlements of the wall." The wall represents either the Torah or the Jewish People. He ran along the battlements, because the battlements are the weakest part of the wall—the base is its strongest part.

If the wall represents Torah, the *Satan* attacks the Torah at its weak point, questioning decrees that have no rational reason like *shaatnez*[17] and *parah adumah*.[18] We know that Satan and the nations taunt Yisrael about these commandments saying, "What is the purpose of this commandment?"

---

17   The prohibition against wearing wool and linen together (Vayikra 19:19)

18   If one came in contact with a corpse, ashes of a red cow were sprinkled on him to purify him from his contamination.

If the wall represents the Jewish People, the battlements refer to the people whose faith and intellect is not very strong.

The rider galloping below on horseback, alludes to the tzaddikim who pursue the mitzvos like race horses.

"He could not catch up with him," means that Hurmin was unable to entice Yisrael because the mitzvos and the Torah protect them from the wiles of the *yetzer hara*.

Since he could not entrap Yisrael, he attacked the nations. This is implied by: "Once they saddled two mules for Hurmin." Rashi explains that the two mules represent two dominant world powers that were incited against each other by Satan. The nations are compared to the mule since it is an imperfect animal. Daniel prophesied (ch.11) that in the end of days the King of the South and the King of the North will attack each other.

"They stood on two bridges across the River Donag"—indicates that they are destined to be annihilated, as it says, *As wax* [donag] *melts before fire* (*Tehillim* 68:3).

"He jumped from one to the other," means, they fought each other, alternately winning and losing, as mentioned in *Daniel*.

"Holding two glasses of wine in his hands, pouring wine from one into the other," refers to the "wine of bewilderment" which the idol worshippers will drink in time to come, as prophesied in *Yeshayah* (51:22). Satan holds two glasses of wine of bewilderment in his hands, referring to the two great world powers that will come to an end in the days of Mashiach.

"Without spilling a drop," suggests that they will be decimated, as it says, *All the wicked of the earth will drain and drink until its dregs* (*Tehillim* 75:9), and nothing will remain of them.

It was a day that, *They rise heavenward,* for in the future, there will be a new heaven and a new earth.

"When the king's agents heard of this," refers to the King of heaven, Who will kill Satan because Satan attempted to entice the tzaddikim, although he was unsuccessful. The Gemara says: In the days of Mashiach, the Holy One, blessed be He, will slaughter the *yetzer hara* in the presence of the tzaddikim and the wicked. To the tzaddikim it will look like a mountain. G-d will wonder: How were the tzaddikim able to overcome [the *yetzer hara*'s allure]? G-d will then slay him, and the *yetzer hara* will no longer influence them, as it says, *I will distance the northern one* [Satan] *from you* (*Yoel* 2:20) (Sukkah 51b).

THE GLORY OF YEHOSHUA

BAVA BASRA 73b

GEMARA: Rabbah bar Bar Chanah continued: I saw a one day-old *re'eim* (antelope) as big as Mount Tabor, which is forty *parsah*s. Its neck was three *parsah*s long; and the resting place of its head was one and a half *parsahs*. It expelled excrement, which clogged the River Yarden.

This metaphor portrays Yehoshua who is compared to a *re'eim* in the verse, *His horns are like the horns of a re'eim* (*Devarim* 33:17).[19]

He is called, "a one day-old *re'eim*," because he was exalted at the beginning of his leadership by conquering thirty-one kings, [as if] goring them with his horns.

Mount Tabor was forty *parsah*s, alluding to the great miracle of the sun standing still for [Yehoshua], which could be seen from as far away as Mount Tabor. The slope of the mountain was forty *parsah*s so that climbing or descending it amounted to twenty *parsah*s. Thus the miracle [of the sun standing still] lasted for as long as it takes to walk twenty *parsahs*, which is 48 hours.

The neck, which denotes strength, was three *parsahs*, symbolizing the army of Yisrael, which covered an area of three *parsahs* by

---

19 In Moshe's blessing to Yosef, the forbearer of Yehoshua.

three *parsahs*. Or it suggests Yerushalayim which is called "the neck" in the verse, *It will pass through Yehudah . . . and reach to the neck* (*Yeshayah* 8:8).

Clogging the River Yarden, refers to the miracle of the splitting of the Yarden River, by Yehoshua.

OPPRESSORS OF YISRAEL

BAVA BASRA 73b

GEMARA: Rabbah bar Bar Chanah further said: I saw a frog as big as the Fort of Hagronia that contained sixty houses. A sea serpent swallowed the frog. Then a raven swallowed the sea serpent and flew up to a tree, sitting there. Imagine how strong that tree must have been! Rav Papa bar Shmuel said: Had I not been there myself, I would not believe it.

J ust like Daniel saw a prophecy of four kingdoms resembling wild beasts that would rule the world, so too, Rabbah bar Bar Chanah saw the world powers that would rule [over Eretz Yisrael] from the time of the second Beis Hamikdash until the coming of Mashiach speedily in our days.

The frog alludes to the Greek empire. It is called a frog because of the [senseless] idolatrous Greek mythology.

The sixty houses, refer to the reign of Alexander [the Great] of Macedonia [who conquered the entire Middle East and the Persian empire].

The sea serpent refers to the Roman empire that defeated Greece. It is called a sea serpent because Rome alludes to the original Serpent [that brought sin into the world], and because of our outrage at the destruction of the Beis Hamikdash [by the Romans], as it says, *The serpent's venom is their wine* (*Devarim* 31:33).

The raven that swallowed the sea serpent, refers to the kingdom of Yishmael [the Arab empire] who is compared to unclean fowl because he is the offspring of Hagar . . .

Sitting in the tree, refers to Yishmael (the Arab nations) conquering Eretz Yisrael in the merit of Avraham whom G-d had promised, *Regarding Yishmael I have heard you: I have blessed him, will make him fruitful, and will increase him most exceedingly and make him a great nation* (*Bereishis* 17:20). Avraham is a mighty tree, as it says, *Avraham planted an* eishel *tree in Beer-sheva* (*Bereishis* 21:33). Look, how great is the merit of this *eishel* tree! Its promise endures; Eretz Yisrael and most of the lands of the dispersion are under [Yishmael's] domination until the day of the Redemption, speedily in our days.

CELEBRATING THE MIRACLE OF PURIM

—————●(())●—————

BAVA BASRA 73b

GEMARA: Rabbah bar Bar Chanah further said: Sailing on a ship, we saw a large fish; a small creeping creature entered its nostrils, [and killed it.] The ocean disgorged the dead fish and dumped it on the shore, destroying sixty cities. Sixty cities ate from its flesh, and sixty cities salted the flesh that remained. From one of its eyeballs three hundred barrels of oil were filled. When we came back after twelve months we saw people sawing its bones into beams to rebuild the destroyed cities.

This tale alludes to the story of Purim.

"We were sailing on a ship," refers to our travails in exile.

The large fish, refers to Haman, who cast lots to determine the month [to destroy the Jews]. The lot fell on the month of Adar whose sign of the stars is "Fish" (Pisces). [Haman] wanted to swallow the Jew like a fish [swallows its prey].

The small creeping creature that entered its nostrils, refers to Mordechai, whom Haman regarded with contempt. But through Mordechai's prayer [Haman] was deposed from his high office and eliminated, symbolized by the dead fish being expelled from the sea.

The sixty cities that were destroyed, refers to the enemies of the Jews they were permitted to destroy, as it says, *to destroy, to kill, and to wipe out the entire army that wants to hurt them* (*Esther* 8:11).

The sixty cities that ate from its flesh, refers to the Jews avenging themselves on their enemies and taking their property. The number sixty is a Talmudic idiom denoting a large quantity.

They filled from its eyeball, refers to Haman who focused his eye on the signs of the zodiac to find the month that would spell misfortune for the Jews, settling on the month of Adar.

The three hundred barrels of oil, refers to the many feasts in the month of Adar [on Purim], as it says, *The Jews had light and gladness, and joy, and honor* (*Esther* 8:16)."

After twelve months people were sawing its bones to rebuild the cities, alluding to the promise of the Jews to rebuild the cities [i.e., the Torah] that Haman wanted to destroy, and to rejoice every year on that day.

The Persian Exile

———◦◉◦———

Bava Basra 73b

GEMARA: Rabbah bar Bar Chanah said further: Traveling on a ship, we saw a fish whose back was

covered with sand, with grass growing from it.
Thinking it was land, we debarked and baked and
cooked on its back. When its back became hot,
the fish flipped over; had our ship not been close
by, we would have drowned.

T he Jewish people are sailors, traveling on the sea of their long
and anguished exile. Only through our prayers and by the
grace of G-d are we saved from drowning and sinking to the bottom of the sea, as our sages say, "Most sailors are pious [because
their daily peril causes them to turn to G-d for help] (Kiddushin
82a)."

The fish, refers to the constellation "Fish" (Pisces) of Adar,
which is the month between the winter, [which suggests the exile,]
and Nissan, the beginning of summer, which suggests [Pesach and]
Redemption. [This month] hints to the relaxing of the exile in the
kingdom of [Persia] and Media [at the time of Purim.]

The fish sprouted grass and appeared as an island, because we
saw the zodiac sign of the "Fish" (Pisces) and thought we were no
longer in exile, since it was close to the time of redemption. We
baked and cooked on its back, because, thinking they were no
longer in exile, the Jews mingled with the non-Jews partaking of
the banquet of Achashveirosh.

The back of the fish became hot, since the decree to annihilate
the Jews was issued in Nissan, the month the weather becomes hot,
as it says, *The king's secretaries were called on the thirteenth day of
Nissan, and they wrote everything exactly as Haman ordered them . . .
to destroy, to kill, and to wipe out all the Jews . . . (Esther 3:12, 13)*

Had we not repented as directed by Mordechai, symbolized by
returning to the ship, we would have drowned in the sea of exile.

MORDECHAI AND ESTHER

BAVA BASRA 73b

GEMARA: Rabbah bar Bar Chanah further said: We traveled aboard a ship, sailing for three days and three nights going from the fin [at the head of a huge fish] to the fin [at its tail]. The fish swam upwards [against the wind], while we sailed downward [with the wind]. Rav Dimi said the ship was traveling so fast that it traveled sixty *parsah* in the time it takes to heat up a kettle of water; indeed we were quicker than an arrow shot by a soldier. Rav Ashi said this fish, which has two fins, was [one of the smaller fishes].

This also, refers to the Jews wandering in exile in the days of Haman in the month of Adar which reaches ascendancy under the sign of Fish (Pisces).

Fins cutting through the sea, signify destruction, and indeed the Jews [in exile] suffered persecution after persecution. Traveling between the two fins symbolized two options for destruction—either the destruction of the Jews, or the destruction of Amalek at the hand of the Jews. Sailing for three days and three nights, refers to their repentance on Esther's command, *Fast for me. Do not eat or drink for three days, night and day* (*Esther* 4:15).

The fish swimming upward refers to Haman rising [to prominence]. We were sailing downward, since we were headed for destruction. However, [through our repentance,] this was turned around, and Haman was raised upward to hang on the gallows, while Mordechai was lowered and saved from the gallows.

THE PLAIN AND THE MYSTICAL MEANINGS
OF THE TORAH

BAVA BASRA 73b

GEMARA: Rabbah bar Bar Chanah also said: We sailed aboard a ship, and saw a bird standing up to its ankles in water with its head reaching the sky. Thinking the water was shallow, we wanted to cool ourselves in it. A heavenly voice rang out, "Don't go down there! A carpenter dropped his hatchet here seven years ago, and it has still not reached bottom; though the water is not deep, the current is very strong."

The bird with its ankles in water and head reaching the sky represents two aspects of the Torah,—its plain meaning (*p'shat*), and its profound mystical connotation (*sod*).

The Torah is compared to a kosher bird, in the following Gemara: The Torah was given in forty days, and the soul is formed in forty days:[20] If one keeps the Torah, one's soul is kept, but if one does not keep the Torah one's soul is not kept. A Tanna taught: We can liken this to one who entrusted a swallow[21] to the care of his servant, saying: "Do not think that if you let it die I will take an *issur*[22] from you. Rather, I will take your soul!" (Menachos 99b). This is because the sound of learning Torah is like the chirping of a bird. Therefore a *metzora*[23] must offer two birds for his purification. The voice of the Torah [symbolized by the birds] atones for the voice he used to speak *lashon hara*—tale-bearing, gossip, and slander.

---

[20] The soul is implanted in the embryo forty days after conception.
[21] Some swallows are kosher birds (*Negaim* 14:1, *Yorah De'ah* 82:7)
[22] A small coin.
[23] One afflicted with leprous marks.

The bird was up to its ankles in water, representing the re-vealed interpretation of the Torah, understood here on earth.

Its head reached the sky, representing the mystical interpreta-tion of the Torah, the esoteric matters of Heaven [like angels and the Throne of Glory] as described in the Works of the Chariot (the first chapter of *Yechezkel*).

We sought to enter the shallow water, thinking that the re-vealed portion of the Torah, is easy to understand. However, a heavenly voice said, "Don't go down there!" Don't take [learning the revealed portions of the Torah] lightly, studying it without the guidance of a teacher.

"A carpenter dropped his hatchet seven years ago, and it has still not reached bottom." The "carpenter" refers to a Torah schol-ar who questioned a halachic point, and has still not found an an-swer after seven years.

"Though the water is not deep, the current is very strong." The subject matter is not so wide-ranging, but the matter is so pro-found that a person who is not thoroughly familiar with the topic cannot penetrate its essence.

GEESE, SYMBOL OF WISDOM

———◈———

BAVA BASRA 73b

GEMARA: Rabbah bar Bar Chanah further said: Traveling in the desert, we saw geese so fat their feathers fell out and streams of fat dripped from them. I asked them, "Will we have a portion of you in the World to Come [when the *tzaddikim* will partake of a lavish feast?]" One goose raised its wing, while another raised its thigh. When I came before Rabbi Elazar, he said to me: "Yisrael will be held accountable for the suffering of these geese.

The Gemara says: If one dreams of geese he may look forward to wisdom (Berachos 57b), for it says, *Wisdom sings out in the street* (*Mishlei* 1:20). We see from here that the honking of a goose symbolizes wisdom.

In the days of Mashiach, wisdom and knowledge will flourish, for everyone—young and old—will have knowledge of G-d. They will walk in the desert to acquire discernment as our forefathers did. G-d will give them geese to eat, in order that they acquire spirituality and insight, just as He gave quail to the tzaddikim in the wilderness for the same purpose. The dripping fat signifies the spiritual delight they will derive from this knowledge. Rabbah bar Bar Chanah, who was a Torah scholar, asked if he would partake from this delight in the future. By raising their wings and thighs the geese indicated to him that acquiring knowledge is not sufficient; one must also do actions of mitzvah, with one's hands and feet.

Rabbi Elazar said: "Yisrael will be held accountable for the suffering of these geese." There will be many Jews who will not do mitzvah actions and will be sinful and rebellious. G-d will take them to task for eating these geese to satisfy their lust, just as He punished our forefathers who ate the quail only to satiate their cravings (*Bamidbar* 11:30-35).

CHANGING ONE'S MAZAL

---·◈·---

BAVA BASRA 74a

GEMARA: Rabbah bar Bar Chanah said: An Arab merchant said, "Let me show you where heaven and earth touch." Following him, I saw many windows. I took my breadbasket and placed it in one of the windows of heaven, [and prayed]. After praying, I looked for the basket but could not find

it. I said to the Arab: "There are thieves here." He
said, "It is the rotating heavenly belt [of the zodiac that moved your basket]. Wait until tomorrow,
and you will find it."

[**H**eaven, refers to a person's fate determined by his
mazal—his sign of the stars. Earth, refers to one's
deeds.]

This allegory can be understood in light of the verse, *Kindness
and Truth have met, Righteousness and Peace have kissed* (*Tehillim*
85:11). Kindness refers to one's mazal, which is bestowed upon
him from the stars. If he practices truth is this world he will have
good fortune despite his astrological signs, thus *kindness and truth*
have met. So too, if one brings peace through his actions on earth,
it will affect the influence of Righteousness from the planet Jupiter.
The two have kissed, joining forces to bring good fortune through
man's good deeds.

The place heaven and earth touch is the point where man's
good deeds and prayer "kiss" heaven [changing] his *mazal* for
good.

Rabbi bar Bar Chanah said: I used to travel across the desert to
earn a livelihood. But changing my mind, I tried a different ap-
proach. I took my breadbasket [i.e., my livelihood] and placed it in
a window of heaven, relying on heaven to provide my sustenance,
and change my *mazal*.

However, even after praying, I could not find my basket. I as-
sumed there must be thieves who stole the sustenance sent to me
from heaven, or perhaps someone stole my prayer so it did not
reach heaven, for my request for sustenance was not answered.

I was told, "the rotating heavenly belt—your [ill-starred]
mazal—is holding back your livelihood. Wait until tomorrow and
you will find it." Tomorrow your *mazal* will change through your
prayers and good deeds, and you will find sustenance in abun-
dance.

Exile Under Christians and Moslems

———=•◆•=———

BAVA BASRA 74b

GEMARA: Rabbi Yehudah Hindo'ah related: Traveling aboard a ship, we came upon a precious stone surrounded by a sea monster. A diver went down to retrieve it. The sea monster came and wanted to swallow the ship. A raven bit off its head, and the water became bloody. A second sea monster came. It took the precious stone and hanging it on the dead monster it came back to life. The first sea monster tried to swallow the ship again, and the raven bit off its head once more, then threw the precious stone into the ship. We had salted birds [for food]. [Experimenting], we placed the precious jewel on them, and they came to life. They took the stone and flew off with it.

The interpretation of this allegory is as follows: Our generation and the generations before us have suffered from the edicts of the Christian Church, which forbids us to learn Torah and perform mitzvos. G-d rescues us in roundabout ways, such as other nations attacking the Romans, which brings about the lifting of the ban. Rabbah bar Bar Chanah was referring to the wars between Christianity and Islam.

Our travels on a ship, refers to our exile among the Christian nations. The precious stone is the Torah, which is more precious than pearls. It was surrounded by a sea monster, referring to the Church, which acts like the primordial Serpent in its barbaric treatment of the Jewish people. The diver who tried to retrieve the stone, refers to Torah scholars who swim in the sea of the Talmud. The sea monster, who wanted to swallow the whole ship, is the Church that issued evil decrees, forbidding us to learn Torah. The raven is the Moslem nations who are compared to a female raven. It bit off the head of the serpent, and the water turned bloody in the ensuing religious wars. Possibly this refers to the killing of Torah scholars by the Christians and Moslems.

The second sea monster who used the precious stone to bring life, refers to righteous gentiles, such as Antoninus[24] and others like him, who learned Torah and merited life in the World to Come. The returning of the sea monster, refers to the Greek empire which enacted evil decrees. The raven bit off its head again, because the Moslem nations waged war against the Greeks, abolishing the evil decrees. The precious stone was thrown into the ship, by the Arab rulers, who in general were kind and permitted the Jews to live by the Torah and practice the mitzvos.

The dead birds, refer to the Torah scholars who suffered incredible hardship and seemed to have perished in the bitter exile. However, they were preserved as if they were salted, since they resisted temptation, and did not violate the Torah.

The birds flew away with the precious stone, means they survived the expulsions and persecutions in the Christian nations, and taking the Torah with them moved to the Moslem countries where they were safe from the evil decrees [of the Church]. May G-d help us until the coming of Mashiach, speedily in our days.

PRAYER AND SUPPLICATION

BAVA BASRA 123a

GEMARA: [Yaakov told his son Yosef], *In addition to what your brothers shall share, I am giving you a*

---

[24] A Roman emperor, who was a close friend and admirer of Rabbi Yehudah Hanasi (*Avodah Zarah* 11a). Antoninus became a *ger tzedek* who will come back to life at *techias hameisim*

portion, which I took from the Amorite with my
sword and bow (Bereishis 48:22). Did he actually
take it with his sword and his bow? After all, it already said, For I do not trust in my bow, neither can
my sword save me! (Tehillim 44:7). [The verse must
refer to spiritual weapons], my sword means "my
prayer" and my bow means "my supplication".

The verse uses the words sword and bow as metaphors for
prayer and supplication. Prayer is referred to as sword because Yaakov's prayer counteracts the blessing given to Eisav, You
shall live by your sword (27:39). [This is implied in the verse, when]
the voice [of prayer] is Yaakov's voice, the hands [will not be] the
hands of Eisav (Bereishis 27:22). Supplication is referred to as bow
because it counteracts the blessing given to Yishmael, He became
an accomplished archer (21:20). Possibly, supplication is referred to
as my bow, because the Hebrew word for my bow is bekashti, which
is similar to the word bakashah, which means supplication, as in,
and my people with my petition [bevakashasi] (Esther 7:3).

The Midrash (Bereishis Rabbah) explains my sword and my bow
to refer to "mitzvos and good deeds." But Rashi on the Torah interprets my sword and my bow as referring to "wisdom and prayer."
I do not understand why he interprets this differently than both the
Gemara and the Midrash.

MAN AS AN ANGEL

BAVA BASRA 164b

GEMARA: There are three transgressions no man can
avoid committing every day: Immoral thoughts,
concentrating on his prayers, and tale bearing.

One may ask: If it is impossible to avoid these transgressions, how can they be considered transgressions? Furthermore, what difference does it make to us that no one can avoid these transgressions?

Possibly we can answer in this manner: The term *adam*—man—denotes a being that is a blend of the spiritual beings of the higher world and the mortals of the lower world. The *Midrash* says: G-d said, "I will create man partly from the upper world and partly from the lower world. If he is found deserving, he will be of the upper world, if not, he will be of the lower world." Idol worshippers are not deserving, thus they are from the lower world and not worthy to be called *adam*—man. Indeed the Gemara says: You [Yisrael] are called *adam,* whereas idol worshippers are not called *adam* (Bava Metzia 114b). Yisrael is worthy and from the higher world, as it says, *I will grant you strides among these [angels] who are standing here* (*Zechariah* 4:6). Our sages also taught: If the rebbi is like an angel of G-d, seek to learn Torah from him (*Moed Katan* 17a). We see that a person should strive to be like an angel of G-d. When the Gemara speaks of three transgressions that no *adam*—man—can avoid, it is referring to a man who does not aspire to emulate the ways of an angel. He is an earthly [physical] *adam*. In fact, the word *adam* is [the acronym of the initials of] *afar va'eifer* (dust and ashes), *dam* (blood), and *marah* (gall). In his physical aspect an *adam* who is of the lower beings, a creature of dust and ashes, cannot concentrate and properly meditate on his prayers. His raging blood, impels him to sin [through immorality]. His gall, incites him to tale bearing, slander and bad character traits. But a person who strives to follow in the ways of the angels, can surely avoid these transgressions; it is therefore appropriate to speak of them as transgressions.

GLOSSARY

ADAR - The twelfth Hebrew month

AGGADAH pl. *AGGADOS* - Homiletic discourses

AMORAH - Talmudic Scholar

B'NEI YISRAEL - Children of Israel

BARAISA pl. *BARAISOS* - outside text, not included in the Mishnah

BEIS HAMIDRASH - Torah study hall

BEIS HAMIKDASH - Holy Temple

BERACHAH pl. *BERACHOS* - blessing

CHAMETZ - leavened bread

CHASSAN - groom

CHAZZAN - leader of the prayer service

CHUPPAH - canopy for marriage ceremony

EICHAH - The Book of Lamentations

EISAV - Esau

ELIYAHU - Elijah

ELOHIM - God

ERETZ YISRAEL - The Land of Israel

GALUS - exile

GAN EDEN - The garden of Eden

GEMARA - Talmud

GEMATRIA - numerical value of a word

HAGGADAH - the text recited at the Passover Seder

HALACHAH - pl. halachos - law

HASHEM - God

IYOV - Job

KALLAH - bride

KAREIS - punishment of premature death

KEDUSHAH - sanctity

KIDDUSH - a declaration sanctifying the beginning of a holy day

KOHEIN pl. *KOHANIM* - Priests, descendants of Aaron

LUCHOS - tablets containing the Ten Commandments
LULAV - palm branch take on Sukkos
MASHIACH - The Messiah
MATZAH pl. *MATZOHS* - unleavened bread
MAZAL - one's astrological forcast
MESECHTA pl. *MESECHTOS* - Tractate
MISHNAH pl. *MISHNAYOS* - compilation of the oral tradition;
       it also refers to one paragraph of this compilation
MITZVAH pl. *MITZVOS* - commandment
MOSHE RABBEINU - Moses our Teacher
MUSSAF - the additional prayer on holidays
NAVI - prophet
PESACH - Passover
SEDER NEZIKIN - The Order of Damages, a portion of the
       Talmud dealing with monetary issues
SEFER - book or scroll
SHABBOS - The day of rest - Saturday
SHAVUOS - Festival of Weeks
SHECHINAH - Divine Presence
SHEMONEH ESREI - the eighteen beracha prayer that we say
       thrice each day
SHOFAR - Ram's horn blown on Rosh Hashana
SUKKAH - hut used on Sukkos
SUKKOS - Festival of Tabernacles
TALMIDEI CHACHAMIM - Torah Scholars
TEFILLAH - prayer
TESHUVAH - repentance
TISHREI - The month containing Rosh Hashannah
TOSAFOS - Supplementary commentary to the Talmud
TUMAH - ritual impurity
TZADDIK pl. *TZADDIKIM* - Pious Person
YAMIM TOVIM - holidays
YETZER HARA - evil inclination
YISRAEL - Israel
YOEL - Joel